P9-CFN-010

most loved recipe collection most loved recipe collection

most loved salads & dressings

Pictured on front cover:
Mixed Green Salad With Grilled Peppers, page 43

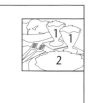

Pictured on back cover:
1. Parfait Crab Salad, page 18
2. Cucumber Avocado Salad, page 16

Most Loved Salads & Dressings
Copyright © Company's Coming Publishing Limited

All rights reserved worldwide. No part of this book may be reproduced, stored in a retrieval system or transmitted in any form by any means without written permission in advance from the publisher.

In the case of photocopying or other reprographic copying, a license may be purchased from the Canadian Copyright Licensing Agency (Access Copyright). Visit www.accesscopyright.ca or call toll free 1-800-893-5777. In the United States, please contact the Copyright Clearance Centre at www.copyright.com or call 978-646-8600.

Brief portions of this book may be reproduced for review purposes, provided credit is given to the source. Reviewers are invited to contact the publisher for additional information.

Second Printing March 2006

Library and Archives Canada Cataloguing in Publication
Paré, Jean, date
Most loved salads & dressings / by Jean Paré.
(Most loved recipe collection)
Includes index.
ISBN 1-896891-94-2
1. Salads. 2. Salad dressing. I. Title. II. Title: Most loved salads and dressings. III. Series.
TX740.P3455 2006   641.8'3   C2005-904191-9

Published by
Company's Coming Publishing Limited
2311 – 96 Street
Edmonton, Alberta, Canada T6N 1G3
Tel: 780-450-6223   Fax: 780-450-1857
www.companyscoming.com

Company's Coming is a registered trademark owned by Company's Coming Publishing Limited

Printed in Canada

We gratefully acknowledge the following suppliers for their generous support of our Test Kitchen and Photo Studio:

Broil King Barbecue®
Corelle®
Hamilton Beach® Canada
Lagostina®
Proctor Silex® Canada
Tupperware®

Our special thanks to the following businesses for providing extensive props for photography:

Anchor Hocking Canada
Canhome Global
Casa Bugatti
Cherison Enterprises Inc.
Chintz & Company
Danesco Inc.
Emile Henry
Island Pottery Inc.
Klass Works
La Cache
Le Gnome
Linens 'N Things
Mikasa Home Store
Out of the Fire Studio
Pfaltzgraff Canada
Pier 1 Imports
Sears Canada
Stokes
The Bay
The Dazzling Gourmet
Tile Town
Totally Bamboo
Tupperware®
Wal-Mart Canada Inc.
Wiltshire®
Winners
X/S Wares
Zenari's

Pictured from left: Orange Almond Salad, page 39; Summer Fruit Salad, page 78; Martini Dressing, page 108; Warm Chicken Salad, page 46

table of contents

the Company's Coming story

"never share a recipe you wouldn't use yourself"

Jean Paré (pronounced "jeen PAIR-ee") grew up understanding that the combination of family, friends and home cooking is the best recipe for a good life. From her mother, she learned to appreciate good cooking, while her father praised even her earliest attempts in the kitchen. When Jean left home, she took with her a love of cooking, many family recipes and an intriguing desire to read cookbooks as if they were novels!

In 1963, when her four children had all reached school age, Jean volunteered to cater the 50th Anniversary of the Vermilion School of Agriculture, now Lakeland College, in Alberta, Canada. Working out of her home, Jean prepared a dinner for more than 1,000 people, which launched a flourishing catering operation that continued for over 18 years. During that time, she had countless opportunities to test new ideas with immediate feedback—resulting in empty plates and contented customers! Whether preparing cocktail sandwiches for a house party or serving a hot meal for 1,500 people, Jean Paré earned a reputation for good food, courteous service and reasonable prices.

As requests for her recipes mounted, Jean was often asked the question, "Why don't you write a cookbook?" Jean responded by teaming up with her son, Grant Lovig, in the fall of 1980 to form Company's Coming Publishing Limited. The publication of *150 Delicious Squares* on April 14, 1981 marked the debut of what would soon become one of the world's most popular cookbook series.

The company has grown since those early days when Jean worked from a spare bedroom in her home. Today, she continues to write recipes while working closely with the staff of the Recipe Factory, as the Company's Coming test kitchen is affectionately known. There she fills the role of mentor, assisting with the development of recipes people most want to use for everyday cooking and easy entertaining. Every Company's Coming recipe is *kitchen-tested* before it's approved for publication.

Jean's daughter, Gail Lovig, is responsible for marketing and distribution, leading a team that includes sales personnel located in major cities across Canada. In addition, Company's Coming cookbooks are published and distributed under licence in the United States, Australia and other world markets. Bestsellers many times over in English, Company's Coming cookbooks have also been published in French and Spanish.

Familiar and trusted in home kitchens around the world, Company's Coming cookbooks are offered in a variety of formats. Highly regarded as kitchen workbooks, the softcover Original Series, with its lay-flat plastic comb binding, is still a favourite among readers.

Jean Paré's approach to cooking has always called for *quick and easy recipes* using *everyday ingredients.* That view has served her well. The recipient of many awards, including the Queen Elizabeth Golden Jubilee medal, Jean was appointed a Member of the Order of Canada, her country's highest lifetime achievement honour.

Jean continues to gain new supporters by adhering to what she calls The Golden Rule of Cooking: *"Never share a recipe you wouldn't use yourself."* It's an approach that works— *millions of times over!*

foreword

For many of us, our first salads were simple mixtures of iceberg lettuce and cucumber, with a few tomato slices for colour. A dollop of bottled dressing finished the dish. It was fast and simple, but hardly the highlight of a meal.

Don't get me wrong; I'm all in favour of simplicity. But when a salad is spectacular, it moves from side-show status to main-stage attraction, and *Most Loved Salads & Dressings* offers everything you need to toss together a show-stopper. How can you miss with a Cranberry Brie or a Bean And Cashew Salad? What about some Minted Pita Chips or Tomato Pesto Croutons tossed on top? *Most Loved Salads & Dressings* invites you to explore the flavours and textures of familiar favourites and some fresh new hits.

Whether it's tossed or molded, marinated or layered, the salads featured here will have friends and family asking for more. Treat them to twists on old themes such as Pesto Pasta and Potato Mint. Rediscover the classics such as Caesar, Greek and Green Goddess, or try new tastes with a Peanut Rice Noodle or Japanese Cabbage Salad. The classics are here too. All-time favourites like Main Macaroni, Overnight Coleslaw and Crispy Cukes await—some things will never go out of style!

Experiment with your favourite greens and dress them for success with delicious homemade dressings such as Blue Cheese, Buttermilk and Italian, or try out-of-the-ordinary mixtures of Apple Spice, Poppy Seed and Creamy Horseradish. Then finish with flair with tasty toppers such as Roasted Pecans or kid-pleasing Little Dilled Snacks.

As our own special topper, all the interesting things we've learned about salads are sprinkled throughout *Most Loved Salads & Dressings*, inviting you to discover the finer points of your favourite salad and dressing ingredients. The possibilities in *Most Loved Salads & Dressings* are endless. Like the other cookbooks in our Most Loved Recipe Collection, it will help you bring exciting colour, flavour and variety to your table.

Jean Paré

nutrition information

Each recipe is analyzed using the most current version of the Canadian Nutrient File from Health Canada, which is based on the United States Department of Agriculture (USDA) Nutrient Database.

- If more than one ingredient is listed (such as "hard margarine or butter"), or if a range is given (1 – 2 tsp., 5 – 10 mL), only the first ingredient or first amount is analyzed.

- For meat, poultry and fish, the serving size per person is based on the recommended 4 oz. (113 g) uncooked weight (without bone), which is 2 – 3 oz. (57 – 85 g) cooked weight (without bone)—approximately the size of a deck of playing cards.

- Milk used is 1% M.F. (milk fat), unless otherwise stated.

- Cooking oil used is canola oil, unless otherwise stated.

- Ingredients indicating "sprinkle," "optional," or "for garnish" are not included in the nutrition information.

Margaret Ng, B.Sc. (Hon.), M.A.
Registered Dietitian

Julienned meats are a must in a traditional chef's salad. Serve with bread for a satisfying meal.

variation

For individual salads, arrange the lettuce on 6 dinner plates. Scatter the cheese, meats and vegetables over top. Arrange the egg wedges on each plate and drizzle salads with dressing. Serves 6.

tip

To remove the core from a head of iceberg lettuce, hit the core end sharply against the countertop to loosen. The core will then easily twist out.

Chef's Salad

Head of iceberg lettuce, chopped or torn	1	1
Grated medium Cheddar cheese	1 cup	250 mL
Julienned deli chicken (see Note)	1 cup	250 mL
Julienned deli ham	1 cup	250 mL
Sliced celery	1 cup	250 mL
Cold cooked peas	1/2 cup	125 mL
Grated carrot	1/4 cup	60 mL
Cherry tomatoes, halved	12	12
Green onions, sliced	6	6
Large hard-cooked eggs, each cut into 4 wedges	6	6
CHEF'S DRESSING		
Mayonnaise (or salad dressing)	1 cup	250 mL
White vinegar	2 tbsp.	30 mL
Granulated sugar	1 tbsp.	15 mL
Paprika	1 tsp.	5 mL
Salt	1 tsp.	5 mL
Pepper	1/4 tsp.	1 mL

Arrange lettuce on large serving platter.

Scatter next 8 ingredients over top.

Arrange egg wedges around edge of platter.

Chef's Dressing: Combine all 6 ingredients in small bowl. Let stand for 2 to 3 minutes until sugar is dissolved. Stir. Makes about 1 1/3 cups (325 mL) dressing. Drizzle over salad. Serves 6.

1 serving: 568 Calories; 47.8 g Total Fat (23.1 g Mono, 12.1 g Poly, 10.2 g Sat); 296 mg Cholesterol; 10 g Carbohydrate; 2 g Fibre; 25 g Protein; 1169 mg Sodium

Pictured on page 7.

Note: To julienne meat, cut into very thin strips that resemble matchsticks.

A contribution to the salad world from Hollywood, California, that's sure to make you famous with family and friends!

about watercress

Watercress is an aquatic plant with thin, crisp stems and small, glossy, dark green leaves. Its slightly bitter, peppery flavour will put zing in your salads and a delicious accent in your sandwiches. Watercress is available in the produce section of your grocery store. For optimum freshness, place the stems in a glass of water, cover with a plastic bag, and store in the refrigerator for up to 2 days. Be sure to remove the stems and wash the leaves well before using.

Cobb Salad

BLUE COBB DRESSING

Olive (or cooking) oil	2/3 cup	150 mL
White vinegar	1/3 cup	75 mL
Crumbled blue cheese (about 1 1/4 oz., 35 g)	1/4 cup	60 mL
Dry mustard	1/2 tsp.	2 mL
Granulated sugar	1/2 tsp.	2 mL
Salt	1 tsp.	5 mL
Pepper	1/4 tsp.	1 mL
Garlic powder	1/8 tsp.	0.5 mL
Head of green leaf lettuce, chopped or torn	1	1
Watercress, stems removed, chopped	1 cup	250 mL
Large hard-cooked eggs	3	3
Bacon slices, cooked crisp and crumbled	8	8
Cubed cooked chicken	2 1/2 cups	625 mL
Ripe medium avocado, diced	1	1
Large tomato, finely chopped	1	1
Green onions, sliced	4	4

Blue Cobb Dressing: Combine first 8 ingredients in small bowl (see Note). Makes about 1 1/4 cups (300 mL) dressing.

Put lettuce and watercress into large bowl. Drizzle 1/3 cup (75 mL) dressing over greens. Toss.

Remove yolks from eggs. Chop yolks finely. Grate egg whites.

Put egg yolk, egg white and remaining 5 ingredients in individual piles or rows on top of greens. Serve with remaining dressing. Serves 6.

1 serving: 533 Calories; 44.3 g Total Fat (23.5 g Mono, 10.4 g Poly, 7.3 g Sat); 175 mg Cholesterol; 8 g Carbohydrate; 3 g Fibre; 27 g Protein; 712 mg Sodium

Pictured on page 9.

Note: If preferred, put the blue cheese on top of the greens instead of in the dressing.

This main dish salad looks lovely served on a platter, but may also be arranged in a pretty glass bowl for an equally attractive presentation.

making the perfect hard-cooked egg

Follow this simple method to help prevent a grey-green ring from forming around the yolk. Place eggs in a single layer in a saucepan. Add cold water until it's about 1 inch (2.5 cm) above the eggs. Cover. Bring to a boil on high. Remove the saucepan from the heat. Let stand, covered, for 20 minutes. Drain. Cover the eggs with cold water. Change the water each time it warms until the eggs are cool enough to handle. Remove the shells.

Niçoise Salad

Head of iceberg lettuce, chopped or torn	1	1
Head of romaine lettuce, chopped or torn	1	1
Sliced cooked, peeled potato	2 cups	500 mL
Cans of white tuna in water (6 1/2 oz., 184 g, each), drained and broken up	2	2
Can of whole green beans, drained and julienned (see Note)	14 oz.	398 mL
Thinly sliced red onion	1 cup	250 mL
Thinly sliced celery	1 cup	250 mL
Sliced ripe olives	1/2 cup	125 mL
PARSLEY VINAIGRETTE		
Olive (or cooking) oil	1/2 cup	125 mL
Chopped fresh parsley (or 1 tbsp., 15 mL, flakes)	1/4 cup	60 mL
Red wine vinegar	3 tbsp.	50 mL
Lemon juice	1 tbsp.	15 mL
Salt	1/2 tsp.	2 mL
Pepper	1/4 tsp.	1 mL
Garlic clove, minced (or 1/4 tsp., 1 mL, powder)	1	1
Medium tomatoes, cut into wedges	2	2
Large hard-cooked eggs, quartered	3	3
Anchovies, drained (optional)	6 – 12	6 – 12

Arrange iceberg and romaine lettuce on large serving platter.

Scatter next 6 ingredients over top.

Parsley Vinaigrette: Combine first 7 ingredients in jar with tight-fitting lid. Shake well. Makes about 2/3 cup (150 mL) dressing. Drizzle over salad.

Arrange tomato and egg wedges around edge of platter. Scatter anchovies over top. Serves 6.

1 serving: 385 Calories; 24.8 g Total Fat (13.4 g Mono, 7 g Poly, 2.8 g Sat); 129 mg Cholesterol; 23 g Carbohydrate; 4 g Fibre; 20 g Protein; 599 mg Sodium

Pictured on page 11.

Note: To julienne green beans, cut into very thin strips that resemble matchsticks.

A classic salad that's a meal in itself. For extra flavour, top with a few sardines or anchovies.

Greek Salad

Head of romaine lettuce, chopped or torn	1	1
Head of iceberg lettuce, chopped or torn	1/2	1/2
English cucumber (with peel), cubed	1	1
Medium tomatoes, cubed	2	2
Cubed feta cheese (about 4 oz., 113 g)	3/4 cup	175 mL
Sliced green onion	1/4 cup	60 mL
Sliced ripe olives (see Note)	1/4 cup	60 mL
GREEK DRESSING		
Olive (or cooking) oil	1/2 cup	125 mL
Red wine vinegar	1/4 cup	60 mL
Chopped fresh parsley (or 1 tbsp., 15 mL, flakes)	1/4 cup	60 mL
Salt	1/2 tsp.	2 mL
Pepper	1/8 tsp.	0.5 mL
Dried oregano	1/8 tsp.	0.5 mL
Garlic powder	1/8 tsp.	0.5 mL

Put romaine and iceberg lettuce into large bowl or arrange on large serving platter.

Scatter next 5 ingredients over top.

Greek Dressing: Combine all 7 ingredients in jar with tight-fitting lid. Shake well. Makes about 3/4 cup (175 mL) dressing. Drizzle over salad. Serves 6.

1 serving: 269 Calories; 24.3 g Total Fat (12.5 g Mono, 6.1 g Poly, 4.4 g Sat); 17 mg Cholesterol; 9 g Carbohydrate; 2 g Fibre; 6 g Protein; 468 mg Sodium

Pictured on page 13.

Note: For a more traditional Greek flavour, use Kalamata olives instead of ripe olives.

Crisp spinach, refreshing strawberries and candied pecans—a must-try combination and a proven favourite in the Company's Coming kitchen.

about balsamic vinegar

Traditional balsamic vinegar, made only from grape must, is aged from 12 to more than 30 years in a series of wooden casks, resulting in a sweet, syrupy liquid that's perfect for salad dressings, meat dishes and desserts. A real treat, traditional balsamic vinegar can cost hundreds of dollars for a tiny bottle!

Commercial balsamic vinegar is a combination of grape must and red wine vinegar with added caramel to mimic the sweetness of traditional balsamic. Inexpensive by comparison, it adds a delicious touch to salad dressings and meat dishes. For best flavour, purchase commercial balsamic vinegar with grape must listed first in the label's ingredient list.

Strawberry Pecan Salad

Pecan pieces	2/3 cup	150 mL
Granulated sugar	1/2 cup	125 mL
Water	1/4 cup	60 mL
Fresh spinach, stems removed, lightly packed	6 cups	1.5 L
Sliced fresh strawberries	2 cups	500 mL
Goat (chèvre) cheese, cut up (optional)	3 oz.	85 g
STRAWBERRY DRESSING		
Olive (or cooking) oil	3 tbsp.	50 mL
Strawberry jam, warmed	2 tbsp.	30 mL
Balsamic vinegar	2 tbsp.	30 mL
Pepper	1/8 tsp.	0.5 mL

Spread pecans in single layer in ungreased shallow pan. Bake in 350°F (175°C) oven for 5 to 10 minutes, stirring or shaking often, until toasted.

Heat and stir sugar and water in small saucepan on low until sugar is dissolved. Bring to a boil on medium-high. Boil gently, uncovered, for 5 to 10 minutes, without stirring, until golden brown. Drizzle over pecans. Let stand for about 20 minutes until cool and hard. Chop.

Arrange spinach on 6 salad plates. Scatter pecan mixture, strawberries and cheese over top of each.

Strawberry Dressing: Combine all 4 ingredients in jar with tight-fitting lid. Shake well. Makes about 1/2 cup (125 mL) dressing. Drizzle over each salad. Serves 6.

1 serving: 269 Calories; 16.7 g Total Fat (9.9 g Mono, 4.6 g Poly, 1.3 g Sat); 0 mg Cholesterol; 31 g Carbohydrate; 4 g Fibre; 3 g Protein; 50 mg Sodium

Pictured on page 15.

Serve this rich-tasting salad with an omelet or quiche for brunch.

about avocados

When is an avocado ripe? Probably not when you buy it! A ripe avocado will yield to gentle pressure when squeezed, but most avocados available in the grocery store are still hard, indicating, like a green banana, the need to sit on the countertop for a few days to ripen. Putting avocados in a paper bag will speed the ripening process.

Ripe, unpeeled avocados will keep in the refrigerator for up to 2 days. For use in salads, sprinkle avocado with a bit of lemon juice or coat well with dressing to prevent it from darkening when exposed to the air.

An attractive salad with vibrant summer colours and a fresh-tasting dressing.

Cucumber Avocado Salad

English cucumber (with peel), thinly sliced diagonally	1	1
Red medium pepper, thinly sliced	1	1
Ripe large avocados, sliced	2	2
Smoked salmon, thinly sliced	4 oz.	113 g
CREAMY LEMON DRESSING		
Sour cream	3 tbsp.	50 mL
Water	2 tbsp.	30 mL
Chopped fresh dill (or 3/4 tsp., 4 mL, dill weed)	1 tbsp.	15 mL
Lemon juice	1 tbsp.	15 mL
Salt	1/4 tsp.	1 mL
Finely chopped red onion	1/4 cup	60 mL
Coarsely chopped capers (optional)	1 tbsp.	15 mL
Freshly ground pepper, for garnish		

Layer first 4 ingredients, in order given, on 4 salad plates.

Creamy Lemon Dressing: Combine first 5 ingredients in small bowl. Makes about 1/3 cup (75 mL) dressing. Drizzle over each salad.

Sprinkle each with onion and capers. Garnish with pepper. Serves 4.

1 serving: 239 Calories; 18.4 g Total Fat (10.7 g Mono, 2.4 g Poly, 3.7 g Sat); 11 mg Cholesterol; 14 g Carbohydrate; 4 g Fibre; 9 g Protein; 388 mg Sodium

Pictured on page 19 and on back cover.

Papaya And Mixed Greens

Mixed salad greens, lightly packed	4 cups	1 L
Medium papaya, seeds reserved, cubed	1	1
Medium tomatoes, seeds removed, cubed	2	2
Chopped green onion	1/4 cup	60 mL

(continued on next page)

MUSTARD DRESSING

Peanut (or cooking) oil	3 tbsp.	50 mL
White wine vinegar	2 tbsp.	30 mL
Reserved papaya seeds	2 tbsp.	30 mL
Liquid honey	1 tbsp.	15 mL
Dry mustard	1 tsp.	5 mL
Salt	1/4 tsp.	1 mL
Pepper, sprinkle		

Arrange salad greens on 6 salad plates.

Scatter papaya, tomato and onion over top of each.

Mustard Dressing: Combine all 7 ingredients in jar with tight-fitting lid. Shake well. Makes about 1/2 cup (125 mL) dressing. Drizzle over each salad. Serves 6.

1 serving: 111 Calories; 7.3 g Total Fat (3.3 g Mono, 2.4 g Poly, 1.2 g Sat); 0 mg Cholesterol; 12 g Carbohydrate; 2 g Fibre; 2 g Protein; 114 mg Sodium

Pictured below.

about mixed salad greens

Mixed salad greens are also known as "mesclun" and are available in bags and bulk in the produce section of your grocery store. This mix of small young greens often includes arugula, curly endive, mizuna, oak leaf, radicchio or sorrel. You can make your own mesclun by combining your favourite types of lettuce with other salad greens.

A layered salad with a novel presentation. These can be made earlier in the day and chilled until serving time.

storing celery

For optimum freshness, store celery in the refrigerator in a perforated plastic bag or in an airtight container equipped with a drip tray. Either container will help keep condensation away from the celery, allowing for a longer shelf life than plastic alone.

Parfait Crab Salad

Large hard-cooked eggs, chopped	2	2
Can of crabmeat (or imitation), drained, cartilage removed, flaked	4 1/4 oz.	120 g
Salad dressing (or mayonnaise)	1/4 cup	60 mL
Sour cream	3 tbsp.	50 mL
Chopped fresh parsley (or 1 tsp., 5 mL, flakes)	1 1/2 tbsp.	25 mL
Milk	1 tbsp.	15 mL
Sweet pickle relish	2 tsp.	10 mL
Finely chopped celery	2 tsp.	10 mL
Salt	1/4 tsp.	1 mL
Onion powder	1/8 tsp.	0.5 mL
Chopped or torn iceberg lettuce, lightly packed	1 cup	250 mL
Green onions, thinly sliced	2	2
Cold cooked peas	1/2 cup	125 mL
Grated medium Cheddar cheese	1/4 cup	60 mL

Combine first 10 ingredients in medium bowl.

Put lettuce into 4 stemmed large parfait glasses (see Note).

Spoon crabmeat mixture on top of lettuce. Layer onion and peas on top of crabmeat mixture.

Sprinkle each with cheese. Chill. Serves 4.

1 serving: *208 Calories; 14.7 g Total Fat (6.4 g Mono, 3.1 g Poly, 4 g Sat); 124 mg Cholesterol; 8 g Carbohydrate; 1 g Fibre; 11 g Protein; 567 mg Sodium*

Pictured on page 19 and on back cover.

Note: If you don't have parfait glasses, large wine glasses or water goblets work equally well.

Top: Parfait Crab Salad, above
Bottom: Cucumber Avocado Salad, page 16

The perfect salad for company! Make it the day before if you like. Just cover it with plastic wrap and chill until ready to serve.

tip

It's always nice to have bacon on hand to add smoky flavour to greens. For ease and convenience, store cooked bacon strips in an airtight container in the freezer. Simply remove as many strips as you need to crumble into salads.

Multi-Layered Salad

Head of iceberg lettuce (see Note), chopped or torn	1	1
Sliced celery	1 cup	250 mL
Large hard-cooked eggs, chopped or sliced	6	6
Cold cooked (or frozen, thawed) peas	1 cup	250 mL
Chopped green pepper	1/2 cup	125 mL
Green onions, sliced	8	8
Can of sliced water chestnuts, drained	8 oz.	227 mL
Bacon slices, cooked crisp and crumbled	8	8
SOUR CREAM DRESSING		
Sour cream	1 cup	250 mL
Salad dressing (or mayonnaise)	1 cup	250 mL
Granulated sugar	2 tbsp.	30 mL
Grated medium Cheddar cheese	1 cup	250 mL
Bacon slices, cooked crisp and crumbled	4	4

Arrange lettuce in bottom of 3 quart (3 L) glass baking dish or large glass bowl.

Layer next 7 ingredients, in order given, on top of lettuce.

Sour Cream Dressing: Combine sour cream, salad dressing and sugar in small bowl. Makes about 2 cups (500 mL) dressing. Spoon on top of salad. Carefully spread dressing to edge of baking dish to seal.

Scatter cheese over dressing. Scatter second amount of bacon over top. Serves 10.

1 serving: 344 Calories; 26.6 g Total Fat (11.9 g Mono, 5.3 g Poly, 7.9 g Sat); 164 mg Cholesterol; 14 g Carbohydrate; 1 g Fibre; 12 g Protein; 431 mg Sodium

Pictured on page 21.

Note: For a more colourful and nutritious salad, use a mixture of iceberg and romaine lettuce plus some spinach leaves.

This large, beautiful salad may be made up to two days ahead. Your guests will love the delicious Mexican flavours and the crunchy texture.

tip

Hot peppers get their fiery heat from the capsaicin contained in their seeds and ribs. Removing the seeds and ribs will reduce the heat. When handling hot peppers, wear rubber gloves and avoid touching your eyes. Remember to wash your hands well afterwards.

Rio Ranchero Layered Salad

Chopped or torn romaine lettuce, lightly packed	8 cups	2 L
Large hard-cooked eggs, sliced	8	8
Halved cherry tomatoes	3 cups	750 mL
Can of black beans, rinsed and drained	19 oz.	540 mL
Green onions, sliced	4	4
Thinly sliced celery	1/2 cup	125 mL
Green medium pepper, diced	1	1
Cans of kernel corn (7 oz., 199 mL, each), drained	2	2
Ripe large avocados, cubed	2	2
Lime juice	1 tbsp.	15 mL
SASSY SALSA DRESSING		
Mayonnaise (or salad dressing)	1 cup	250 mL
Sour cream	1 cup	250 mL
Chunky salsa	2/3 cup	150 mL
Finely chopped fresh parsley (or 2 tbsp., 30 mL, flakes)	1/2 cup	125 mL
Lime juice	1/3 cup	75 mL
Grated lime zest	1/2 tsp.	2 mL
Ground cumin	1/2 tsp.	2 mL
Chili powder	1/2 tsp.	2 mL
Granulated sugar	1/2 tsp.	2 mL
Cherry tomatoes	8	8
Grated sharp Cheddar cheese	3/4 cup	175 mL
Grated Monterey Jack With Jalapeño cheese	3/4 cup	175 mL
Bacon slices, cooked crisp and crumbled (optional)	8	8
Sliced ripe olives	2 tbsp.	30 mL
Diced jalapeño pepper (see Tip)	2 tbsp.	30 mL

(continued on next page)

Put lettuce into extra-large glass bowl. Pack down slightly.

Press some egg slices against inside of bowl to decorate (see photo, page 25). Arrange remaining egg slices in single layer on top of lettuce.

Arrange some tomato halves, cut-side out, against inside of bowl to decorate. Layer remaining tomato halves on top of egg slices and lettuce.

Layer next 5 ingredients, in order given, on top of tomato halves.

Put avocado into small bowl. Drizzle with lime juice. Toss gently until coated. Scatter on top of corn.

Sassy Salsa Dressing: Combine first 9 ingredients in medium bowl. Makes about 3 cups (750 mL) dressing. Spoon on top of avocado. Carefully spread dressing to edge of bowl to seal. Cover with plastic wrap. Chill.

Just before serving, scatter remaining 6 ingredients, in order given, over dressing. Serves 12.

1 serving: 424 Calories; 33.5 g Total Fat (16.2 g Mono, 6.9 g Poly, 8.4 g Sat); 178 mg Cholesterol; 20 g Carbohydrate; 4 g Fibre; 13 g Protein; 430 mg Sodium

Pictured on page 25.

about romaine lettuce

The slightly bitter flavour of these long leaves has made romaine lettuce a popular choice for Caesar salads. But don't let that limit you. Romaine is wonderful used alone, or in combination with other greens, in any leafy salad. For optimum freshness, wrap washed leaves loosely with damp paper towels and put in a plastic bag, or place washed leaves in an airtight container equipped with a drip tray. Store in the refrigerator for up to 5 days.

This salad takes a little more time to prepare, but it's worth it! Fresh corn kernels and roasted peppers liven up crisp greens and add a hint of sweetness to the salad.

about corn on the cob

For maximum flavour and freshness, corn is best eaten the same day it's purchased; even better, the same day it's picked! If that's not convenient, corn may be stored in its husk in the refrigerator. Keep in mind that the longer corn is off the stalk before cooking, the more of its natural sugar will convert to starch, causing gradual lessening of its sweet flavour.

When buying corn, look for cobs with dark green husks and golden brown silk. Although tempting, removing the husks in the grocery store will speed moisture loss from the kernels and should be avoided. Instead, choose ears that have full, rounded tips, indicating that the cobs are mature.

Corn And Tomato Salad

Medium corncobs	2	2
Boiling water		
Green medium peppers, quartered	2	2
Head of romaine lettuce, chopped or torn	1	1
Halved cherry tomatoes	2 cups	500 mL
Thinly sliced red onion	3/4 cup	175 mL
Chopped fresh mint leaves (or 1 tbsp., 15 mL, dried)	1/4 cup	60 mL
SWEET CHILI DRESSING		
Olive (or cooking) oil	1/4 cup	60 mL
Sweet chili sauce	3 tbsp.	50 mL
White wine vinegar	2 tbsp.	30 mL
Garlic clove, minced (or 1/4 tsp., 1 mL, powder)	1	1
Salt	1/4 tsp.	1 mL

Cook corncobs in boiling water in large pot or Dutch oven for 5 to 7 minutes until tender-crisp. Drain. Cool. Cut corn kernels into 2 inch (5 cm) long strips from each cob. Put into large bowl.

Arrange green pepper pieces, skin-side up, on ungreased baking sheet. Broil on top rack in oven for 10 to 15 minutes until skins are blistered and blackened. Transfer to small bowl. Cover with plastic wrap. Let sweat for about 15 minutes until cool enough to handle. Peel and discard skins. Cut into 2 inch (5 cm) strips. Add to corn.

Add next 4 ingredients. Toss gently.

Sweet Chili Dressing: Combine all 5 ingredients in jar with tight-fitting lid. Shake well. Makes about 2/3 cup (150 mL) dressing. Drizzle over salad. Toss gently. Serves 8.

1 serving: 136 Calories; 7.9 g Total Fat (5.5 g Mono, 0.9 g Poly, 1.1 g Sat); 0 mg Cholesterol; 16 g Carbohydrate; 4 g Fibre; 3 g Protein; 174 mg Sodium

Pictured on page 25.

Top left: Rio Ranchero Layered Salad, page 22
Bottom right: Corn And Tomato Salad, above

Spinach salad with a lemon twist. You'll love the tangy dressing!

about spinach

Spinach is available in bags or bunches in the produce section of your grocery store. Store spinach bunches in a perforated plastic bag in the refrigerator for up to 5 days. Wash leaves thoroughly just before using. Although certainly edible, removing the stems will make spinach more attractive for use in salads.

A bountiful salad with a tasty dressing. Sure to please everyone.

Spinach Mushroom Salad

Sliced fresh white mushrooms	2 cups	500 mL
Bag of fresh spinach, stems removed	10 oz.	284 g
Bacon slices, cooked crisp and crumbled	6	6
Sliced green onion	1/3 cup	75 mL
LIGHT LEMON DRESSING		
Egg yolk (large), see Note	1	1
Olive (or cooking) oil	2 tbsp.	30 mL
Lemon juice	2 tbsp.	30 mL
Granulated sugar	1/2 tsp.	2 mL
Salt	3/4 tsp.	4 mL
Pepper	1/8 tsp.	0.5 mL

Put first 4 ingredients into large bowl. Toss.

Light Lemon Dressing: Combine all 6 ingredients in small bowl. Makes about 1/3 cup (75 mL) dressing. Drizzle over salad. Toss well. Serves 8.

1 serving: 81 Calories; 6.7 g Total Fat (3.4 g Mono, 1.5 g Poly, 1.3 g Sat); 31 mg Cholesterol; 3 g Carbohydrate; 1 g Fibre; 3 g Protein; 329 mg Sodium

Pictured on page 27.

Note: Immediately following preparation, salad dressings containing uncooked eggs should be placed in the refrigerator and stored there until serving time.

Tossed Salad

Head of iceberg lettuce, chopped or torn	1	1
Large hard-cooked eggs, chopped	2	2
Sliced fresh white mushrooms	1 cup	250 mL
Chopped English cucumber (with peel)	1/2 cup	125 mL
Sliced celery	1/2 cup	125 mL
Medium tomato, chopped	1	1
Green onions, sliced	4	4
Radishes, sliced	6	6

(continued on next page)

SIMPLE MAYONNAISE DRESSING

Mayonnaise (or salad dressing)	1/2 cup	125 mL
Milk	2 tbsp.	30 mL
Prepared mustard	1 tsp.	5 mL
Granulated sugar	1 tsp.	5 mL

Put first 8 ingredients into large bowl. Toss.

Simple Mayonnaise Dressing: Combine all 4 ingredients in small bowl. Makes about 2/3 cup (150 mL) dressing. Drizzle over salad. Toss well. Serves 8.

1 serving: 148 Calories; 13.4 g Total Fat (7 g Mono, 4.2 g Poly, 1.6 g Sat); 63 mg Cholesterol; 4 g Carbohydrate; 1 g Fibre; 3 g Protein; 119 mg Sodium

Pictured below.

Top: Spinach Mushroom Salad, page 26
Centre right and bottom: Tossed Salad, page 26

A salad that's stood the test of time!

caesar croutons

Heat 2 tbsp. (30 mL) olive (or cooking) oil in a large frying pan on medium. Add 2 cups (500 mL) dry white bread cubes. Sprinkle with garlic salt (for Secret Caesar, omit garlic salt). Heat and stir for about 3 minutes until golden. Remove the croutons to a paper towel-lined plate. Cool.

Caesar Salad

Head of romaine lettuce, chopped or torn	1	1
Grated Parmesan cheese	1/2 cup	125 mL
Caesar Croutons (recipe, left)		
EASY CAESAR DRESSING		
Mayonnaise (or salad dressing)	1 cup	250 mL
Lemon juice	1 tbsp.	15 mL
Worcestershire sauce	1/2 tsp.	2 mL
Garlic clove, minced (or 1/4 tsp., 1 mL, powder)	1	1
Salt	1/4 tsp.	1 mL
Pepper	1/8 tsp.	0.5 mL

Put lettuce, Parmesan cheese and croutons into large bowl. Toss.

Easy Caesar Dressing: Combine all 6 ingredients in small bowl. Makes about 1 cup (250 mL) dressing. Drizzle over salad. Toss well. Serves 6.

1 serving: 401 Calories; 36.5 g Total Fat (19.4 g Mono, 10.9 g Poly, 5.4 g Sat); 30 mg Cholesterol; 12 g Carbohydrate; 2 g Fibre; 7 g Protein; 649 mg Sodium

Pictured on page 29.

When you crave Caesar Salad, but don't care for the strong flavour of fresh garlic, this one's for you. Jean's secret for a more subtle taste is to use garlic powder instead.

variation

For extra good taste, add 1/2 cup (125 mL) crumbled blue cheese to your favourite Caesar salad.

Secret Caesar

Head of romaine lettuce, chopped or torn	1	1
Grated Parmesan cheese	1/4 cup	60 mL
Caesar Croutons (recipe, above left)		
SECRET CAESAR DRESSING		
Egg yolk (large), see Note	1	1
Grated Parmesan cheese	1/2 cup	125 mL
Olive (or cooking) oil	6 tbsp.	100 mL
Red wine vinegar	2 tbsp.	30 mL
Lemon juice	1 tbsp.	15 mL
Worcestershire sauce	1 tsp.	5 mL
Garlic powder	1/4 tsp.	1 mL
Salt	1/4 tsp.	1 mL
Pepper	1/8 tsp.	0.5 mL

(continued on next page)

Put lettuce, Parmesan cheese and croutons into large bowl. Toss.

Secret Caesar Dressing: Combine all 9 ingredients in small bowl. Makes about 3/4 cup (175 mL) dressing. Drizzle over salad. Toss well. Serves 6.

1 serving: 271 Calories; 21.4 g Total Fat (11 g Mono, 4.7 g Poly, 4.5 g Sat); 47 mg Cholesterol; 12 g Carbohydrate; 2 g Fibre; 9 g Protein; 537 mg Sodium

Pictured below.

Note: Immediately following preparation, salad dressings containing uncooked eggs should be placed in the refrigerator and stored there until serving time.

Top right: Caesar Salad, page 28
Bottom right and left: Secret Caesar, page 28

Spicy chicken takes this Caesar from a side to a complete meal.

about "blackened" cooking

"Blackened" cooking originated in New Orleans. Traditionally, meat or fish is rubbed with Cajun spices and then cooked quickly in a hot, greased pan, giving the meat a crispy, dark-coloured crust. In this recipe we've added the spices during cooking to speed preparation, with equally tasty results.

tip

Red and white wine vinegars may be used interchangeably in most salad dressings. A recipe may call for one over the other because each offers a slightly different flavour and colour, much the same as red and white wines. However, as each offers an agreeable tang, feel free to use whichever you have on hand.

Blackened Chicken Caesar Salad

CREAMY CAESAR DRESSING

Grated Parmesan cheese	1/2 cup	125 mL
Olive (or cooking) oil	3 tbsp.	50 mL
Sour cream	3 tbsp.	50 mL
White (or red) wine vinegar	1 tbsp.	15 mL
Lemon juice	1 tsp.	5 mL
Worcestershire sauce	1 tsp.	5 mL
Garlic salt	1/2 tsp.	2 mL
Pepper	1/4 tsp.	1 mL

BLACKENED CHICKEN

Cooking oil	1 tbsp.	15 mL
Boneless, skinless chicken breast halves, cut into 3/4 inch (2 cm) pieces	2 lbs.	900 g
Ketchup	2 tbsp.	30 mL
Paprika	1 tbsp.	15 mL
Salt	2 tsp.	10 mL
Pepper	1/2 tsp.	2 mL
Onion powder	1/2 tsp.	2 mL
Ground thyme	1/2 tsp.	2 mL
Chili powder	1/2 tsp.	2 mL
Cayenne pepper	1/2 tsp.	2 mL
Heads of romaine lettuce, chopped or torn	2	2
Croutons	1 cup	250 mL
Grated Parmesan cheese	1/4 cup	60 mL

Grated Parmesan cheese, for garnish

Creamy Caesar Dressing: Combine first 8 ingredients in small bowl. Makes about 1/2 cup (125 mL) dressing. Chill for 10 minutes to blend flavours.

Blackened Chicken: Heat wok or large frying pan on medium-high until very hot. Add cooking oil. Add chicken. Stir-fry for 6 to 7 minutes until chicken turns white.

(continued on next page)

Add next **8** ingredients. Stir-fry for **8** to **10** minutes until chicken is no longer pink inside. Remove from heat.

Put lettuce, croutons and second amount of Parmesan cheese into large bowl. Toss. Drizzle dressing over salad. Toss. Arrange on **8** dinner plates. Scatter chicken mixture over top of each.

Garnish each with Parmesan cheese. Serves **8**.

1 serving: 290 Calories; 13.9 g Total Fat (6.2 g Mono, 2.9 g Poly, 3.7 g Sat); 75 mg Cholesterol; 9 g Carbohydrate; 2 g Fibre; 32 g Protein; 983 mg Sodium

Pictured below.

This main course salad is a treat served in Tortilla Bowls. If you're strapped for time, toss the salad with broken-up tortilla chips and serve individual portions on brightly coloured plates.

tortilla bowls

Grease the bottom and outside of an ovenproof 2 cup (500 mL) liquid measure. Invert onto a baking sheet. Press a 7 1/2 inch (19 cm) diameter flour tortilla over the bottom and side of the liquid measure. Bake in a 325°F (160°C) oven for 7 to 10 minutes, pressing the tortilla against the measure occasionally, until brown spots appear. Makes 1 tortilla bowl.

Pictured on page 33.

Mexican Salad

Cooking oil	1 tsp.	5 mL
Lean ground beef	1/2 lb.	225 g
Water	1/2 cup	125 mL
Taco seasoning mix, stir before measuring	4 tsp.	20 mL
Shredded iceberg lettuce, lightly packed	4 cups	1 L
Can of pinto beans, rinsed and drained	19 oz.	540 mL
Medium tomato, diced	1	1
Small red pepper, diced	1	1
Very thinly sliced red onion	1 cup	250 mL
Tortilla Bowls (recipe, left)	6	6
CHILI DRESSING		
Plain yogurt	1/2 cup	125 mL
Light sour cream	1/2 cup	125 mL
Chili sauce	3 tbsp.	50 mL
Onion powder	1/2 tsp.	2 mL
Salt	1/4 tsp.	1 mL
Garlic powder	1/8 tsp.	0.5 mL

Heat cooking oil in medium frying pan on medium. Add ground beef. Scramble-fry for about 10 minutes until no longer pink. Drain.

Add water and taco seasoning. Stir. Reduce heat to medium-low. Cook, uncovered, for about 5 minutes, stirring occasionally, until liquid is evaporated. Cool. Transfer to large bowl.

Add next 5 ingredients. Toss.

Spoon salad into Tortilla Bowls.

Chili Dressing: Combine all 6 ingredients in small bowl. Makes about 1 1/4 cups (300 mL) dressing. Drizzle over each salad. Serves 6.

1 serving: 243 Calories; 6.9 g Total Fat (3 g Mono, 0.9 g Poly, 3.4 g Sat); 25 mg Cholesterol; 32 g Carbohydrate; 6 g Fibre; 15 g Protein; 613 mg Sodium

Pictured on page 33.

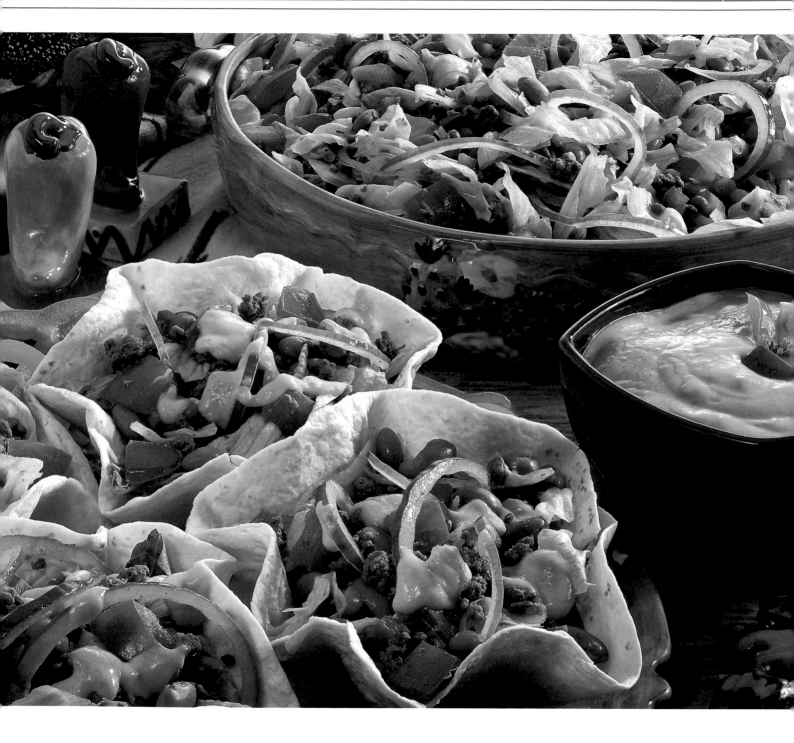

A great addition to any meal. Easy to double for a large crowd.

about iceberg lettuce

Originally called "crisphead," this popular lettuce became known as "iceberg" in the days before modern refrigeration, when shipping boxes were covered with ice to keep the lettuce fresh during transportation. It is also known as "head lettuce" because it grows in round, tightly packed heads. It can be chopped, torn, shredded or cut into wedges, making it one of the most versatile salad greens available. To store, put whole iceberg lettuce in a plastic bag or other airtight container and keep in the refrigerator for up to 2 weeks.

Green Goddess Salad

Head of iceberg lettuce, chopped or torn	1	1
Canned crabmeat (or salad shrimp)	1/2 cup	125 mL
GREEN GODDESS DRESSING		
Salad dressing (or mayonnaise)	1/2 cup	125 mL
Sour cream	1/4 cup	60 mL
Chopped green onion	2 tbsp.	30 mL
Chopped fresh parsley (or 1 1/2 tsp., 7 mL, flakes)	2 tbsp.	30 mL
Anchovy paste	1 tsp.	5 mL
Worcestershire sauce	1/2 tsp.	2 mL
Prepared mustard	1/4 tsp.	1 mL
Garlic powder	1/8 tsp.	0.5 mL
Salt	1/4 tsp.	1 mL
Pepper, sprinkle		

Put lettuce and crabmeat into large bowl. Toss.

Green Goddess Dressing: Combine all 10 ingredients in small bowl. Makes about 1 cup (250 mL) dressing. Drizzle over salad. Toss well. Serves 8 to 10.

1 serving: 110 Calories; 9 g Total Fat (4.6 g Mono, 2.7 g Poly, 1.3 g Sat); 13 mg Cholesterol; 4 g Carbohydrate; 0 g Fibre; 3 g Protein; 274 mg Sodium

Pictured on page 35.

The sweet, smoky dressing tastes so good on simple romaine lettuce. Make the dressing just before serving so that it's still warm.

Warm Bacon Lettuce Salad

Head of romaine lettuce, chopped or torn	1	1
Green onions, chopped	3	3
WARM BACON DRESSING		
Apple cider vinegar	1/4 cup	60 mL
Granulated sugar	2 tbsp.	30 mL
Water	2 tbsp.	30 mL
Salt	1/2 tsp.	2 mL
Pepper	1/4 tsp.	1 mL

(continued on next page)

Bacon slices, diced	5	5
Chopped onion	1/2 cup	125 mL
Large hard-cooked egg, chopped	1	1

Put lettuce and green onion into large bowl. Toss.

Warm Bacon Dressing: Combine first 5 ingredients in jar with tight-fitting lid. Shake well.

Cook bacon and onion in medium frying pan until bacon is almost crisp. Add bacon, onion and drippings to vinegar mixture. Shake well. Makes about 1/2 cup (125 mL) dressing. Drizzle over salad. Toss well.

Sprinkle with egg. Serve immediately. Serves 4.

1 serving: 117 Calories; 5.5 g Total Fat (2.4 g Mono, 0.8 g Poly, 1.8 g Sat); 61 mg Cholesterol; 12 g Carbohydrate; 2 g Fibre; 6 g Protein; 448 mg Sodium

Pictured below.

Top: Green Goddess Salad, page 34
Bottom: Warm Bacon Lettuce Salad, page 34

An inviting summer salad with a light, sweet and sour flavour. Almonds add a perfectly nutty touch.

tip

To toast almonds, spread them in a single layer in an ungreased shallow pan. Bake in a 350°F (175°C) oven for 5 to 10 minutes, stirring or shaking often, until desired doneness.

segmenting oranges

Cut a small slice of peel from both ends so that the flesh is exposed. Place the orange, cut-side down, on a cutting board. Remove the peel with a sharp knife, cutting down and around the flesh, leaving as little pith as possible (photo 1). Over a small bowl, cut on either side of the membranes to release the segments (photo 2).

Fruity Butter Lettuce Salad

Head of butter lettuce, chopped or torn	1	1
Medium oranges, peeled and segmented	2	2
Sliced fresh strawberries	2/3 cup	150 mL
Crumbled feta cheese (about 2 1/2 oz., 70 g)	1/2 cup	125 mL
Sliced almonds, toasted (see Tip)	1/2 cup	125 mL
ORANGE DRESSING		
Olive (or cooking) oil	2 tbsp.	30 mL
Orange juice	2 tbsp.	30 mL
White wine vinegar	1 tbsp.	15 mL
Granulated sugar	2 tsp.	10 mL
Sesame oil, for flavour	1/4 tsp.	1 mL
Salt	1/4 tsp.	1 mL
Pepper, just a pinch		

Put first 5 ingredients into large bowl. Toss gently.

Orange Dressing: Combine all 7 ingredients in jar with tight-fitting lid. Shake well. Makes about 1/3 cup (75 mL) dressing. Drizzle over salad. Toss gently. Serves 6.

1 serving: 171 Calories; 12.7 g Total Fat (7.3 g Mono, 1.7 g Poly, 3.2 g Sat); 12 mg Cholesterol; 12 g Carbohydrate; 3 g Fibre; 5 g Protein; 254 mg Sodium

Pictured on page 37.

Top: Spinach Squash Salad, page 38
Bottom: Fruity Butter Lettuce Salad, page 36

An aromatic salad with rich, autumn colours and a delicate, nutty flavour.

tip

Always dry salad greens thoroughly after washing so that excess water does not dilute the dressing or prevent it from coating the salad.

about butternut squash

A long, straight neck and round bottom give butternut squash its distinct appearance. Its cream-coloured peel is easy to remove, revealing a deep orange flesh. Grilled, baked or steamed, butternut squash adds a sweet, nutty flavour to salads, soups, stews and desserts.

Spinach Squash Salad

Small butternut squash, peeled and cut into 1/8 inch (3 mm) slices	1/2	1/2
Fresh white medium mushrooms, halved	12	12
Thin prosciutto (or back bacon) slices, cooked crisp and broken into 3/4 inch (2 cm) pieces	6	6
Bag of fresh spinach, stems removed	10 oz.	284 g
Shaved Parmesan cheese	1/2 cup	125 mL
APPLE SPICE DRESSING		
Olive (or cooking) oil	1/4 cup	60 mL
Apple cider vinegar	2 tbsp.	30 mL
Garlic clove, minced (or 1/4 tsp., 1 mL, powder)	1	1
Ground nutmeg	1/8 tsp.	0.5 mL
Ground cinnamon	1/8 tsp.	0.5 mL
Salt	1/8 tsp.	0.5 mL
Pepper	1/8 tsp.	0.5 mL

Spray both sides of each squash slice with cooking spray. Preheat electric grill for 5 minutes or gas barbecue to medium (to broil vegetables, see page 42). Cook squash on greased grill for about 5 minutes per side until browned and tender. Transfer to large plate. Cut into 3/4 inch (2 cm) pieces. Put into large bowl.

Spray mushroom halves with cooking spray. Cook on greased grill for about 5 minutes, turning once, until browned. Transfer to large plate. Cut each half into 2 pieces. Add to squash.

Add prosciutto, spinach and Parmesan cheese. Toss gently.

Apple Spice Dressing: Combine all 7 ingredients in jar with tight-fitting lid. Shake well. Makes about 1/3 cup (75 mL) dressing. Drizzle over salad. Toss gently. Serves 4.

1 serving: 307 Calories; 23.6 g Total Fat (14 g Mono, 2.1 g Poly, 6.2 g Sat); 18 mg Cholesterol; 15 g Carbohydrate; 4 g Fibre; 12 g Protein; 536 mg Sodium

Pictured on page 37.

Orange Almond Salad

Head of romaine lettuce, chopped or torn	1	1
Can of mandarin orange segments, drained	10 oz.	284 mL
Slivered almonds, toasted (see Tip)	1/4 cup	60 mL
Green onions, sliced	2	2
SWEET VINAIGRETTE		
Olive (or cooking) oil	1/4 cup	60 mL
White vinegar	1/4 cup	60 mL
Granulated sugar	1/4 cup	60 mL

Put first 4 ingredients into large bowl. Toss gently.

Sweet Vinaigrette: Combine olive oil, vinegar and sugar in jar with tight-fitting lid. Shake well. Makes about 1/2 cup (125 mL) vinaigrette. Drizzle over salad. Toss gently. Serves 4.

1 serving: 268 Calories; 19.3 g Total Fat (11.5 g Mono, 5.4 g Poly, 1.5 g Sat); 0 mg Cholesterol; 23 g Carbohydrate; 3 g Fibre; 4 g Protein; 10 mg Sodium

Pictured below.

Simply delicious. Mandarin oranges add a refreshing flavour to this light salad.

tip

To toast almonds, spread them in a single layer in an ungreased shallow pan. Bake in a 350°F (175°C) oven for 5 to 10 minutes, stirring or shaking often, until desired doneness.

This large salad is perfect for a buffet or summertime barbecue. The savoury dressing has a flavour that is unsurpassed!

about anchovy paste

Anchovy paste is a mixture of crushed anchovies, vinegar, water and spices, and comes in a tube for easy use. Canned anchovies may be mashed with a little bit of the oil from the can for an acceptable substitute.

Chunky Vegetable Salad

SWEET VEGGIE DRESSING

Olive (or cooking) oil	1/3 cup	75 mL
Coarsely chopped onion	1/4 cup	60 mL
Coarsely chopped carrot	1/4 cup	60 mL
Large egg (see Note)	1	1
White wine vinegar	2 tbsp.	30 mL
Granulated sugar	1 tbsp.	15 mL
Garlic cloves, minced (or 1/2 – 3/4 tsp., 2 – 4 mL, powder)	2 – 3	2 – 3
Anchovy paste	2 – 3 tsp.	10 – 15 mL
Dried oregano	1/2 tsp.	2 mL
Paprika	1/2 tsp.	2 mL
Celery seed	1/4 tsp.	1 mL
Salt	1/4 tsp.	1 mL
Pepper	1/8 tsp.	0.5 mL
Capers (optional)	1 tsp.	5 mL
English cucumber (with peel), cubed	1	1
Green medium pepper, cut into 3/4 inch (2 cm) pieces	1	1
Yellow medium pepper, cut into 3/4 inch (2 cm) pieces	1	1
Medium tomatoes, seeds removed, cubed	2	2
Coarsely chopped iceberg lettuce, lightly packed	6 cups	1.5 L
Crumbled feta cheese (about 3 oz., 85 g), optional	2/3 cup	150 mL

Sweet Veggie Dressing: Process first 14 ingredients in blender or food processor for about 2 minutes until smooth. Chill for 30 minutes to blend flavours. Makes about 1 cup (250 mL) dressing.

Put next 4 ingredients into large bowl. Drizzle with dressing. Toss.

(continued on next page)

Add lettuce and cheese. Toss gently. Serves 8.

1 serving: 139 Calories; 10.7 g Total Fat (7.3 g Mono, 1.1 g Poly, 1.6 g Sat); 28 mg Cholesterol;
10 g Carbohydrate; 2 g Fibre; 3 g Protein; 159 mg Sodium

Pictured below.

Note: Immediately following preparation, salad dressings containing uncooked
eggs should be placed in the refrigerator and stored there until serving time.

Clockwise from top left:
Grilled Veggie Salad, page 42
Chunky Vegetable Salad, page 40
Apple And Shrimp Salad, page 44

A bright, colourful salad that's sure to become a favourite! The grilled vegetable portion of this salad may be prepared a day ahead and chilled overnight.

broiling peppers

Peppers may be broiled in the oven instead of grilled. Place cut peppers, skin-side up, on a greased broiler pan. Broil on the top rack for 10 to 15 minutes until skins are blistered and blackened. Transfer to a small bowl. Cover with plastic wrap. Let sweat for about 15 minutes until cool enough to handle. Peel and discard skins.

broiling vegetables

Vegetables may be broiled in the oven instead of grilled. Place vegetables on a greased broiler pan. Broil on the top rack and turn occasionally, until desired doneness.

Grilled Veggie Salad

Red medium pepper, quartered	1	1
Medium zucchini (with peel), cut lengthwise into 1/4 inch (6 mm) slices	1	1
Thinly sliced peeled yam (or sweet potato)	1 cup	250 mL
BALSAMIC DRESSING		
Olive (or cooking) oil	3 tbsp.	50 mL
Balsamic vinegar	2 tbsp.	30 mL
Honey Dijon mustard	1 tbsp.	15 mL
Chopped fresh thyme leaves (or 1/2 tsp., 2 mL, dried)	1 1/2 tsp.	7 mL
Garlic clove, minced (or 1/4 tsp., 1 mL, powder)	1	1
Salt	1/4 tsp.	1 mL
Fresh spinach, stems removed, lightly packed	4 cups	1 L

Preheat electric grill for 5 minutes or gas barbecue to medium (to broil peppers and vegetables, see left). Arrange red pepper pieces, skin-side down, on greased grill. Cook for 10 to 15 minutes until skins are blistered and blackened. Transfer to small bowl. Cover with plastic wrap. Let sweat for about 15 minutes until cool enough to handle. Peel and discard skins. Cut into thin slices. Put into large bowl.

Cook zucchini slices on greased grill for about 5 minutes per side until grill marks appear. Cook yam slices on greased grill for 3 to 5 minutes per side until tender. Transfer to large plate. Cut zucchini and yam slices into bite-size pieces. Add to red pepper.

Balsamic Dressing: Combine first 6 ingredients in jar with tight-fitting lid. Shake well. Makes about 1/2 cup (125 mL) dressing. Drizzle over vegetables. Toss. Cover. Chill for 30 minutes to blend flavours.

Add spinach. Toss well. Serves 4.

1 serving: 174 Calories; 11 g Total Fat (7.6 g Mono, 1.2 g Poly, 1.5 g Sat); 0 mg Cholesterol; 18 g Carbohydrate; 5 g Fibre; 3 g Protein; 253 mg Sodium

Pictured on page 41.

Mixed Green Salad With Grilled Peppers

A variety of vibrant vegetables make this an eye-appealing salad.

Red medium pepper, quartered	1	1
Yellow medium pepper, quartered	1	1
Croutons (recipe, right)		
Bags of mixed salad greens (4 1/2 oz., 128 g, each)	2	2
Can of romano beans, rinsed and drained	19 oz.	540 mL
Kalamata olives	1/2 cup	125 mL
Red medium onion, halved and thinly sliced	1	1
BASIL DRESSING		
Olive (or cooking) oil	1/3 cup	75 mL
Chopped fresh basil	3 tbsp.	50 mL
Red wine vinegar	2 tbsp.	30 mL
Garlic clove, minced (or 1/4 tsp., 1 mL, powder)	1	1
Granulated sugar	1 tsp.	5 mL
Salt	1/4 tsp.	1 mL
Pepper	1/8 tsp.	0.5 mL

Preheat electric grill for 5 minutes or gas barbecue to medium (to broil peppers, see page 42). Arrange red and yellow pepper pieces, skin-side down, on greased grill. Cook for 10 to 15 minutes until skins are blistered and blackened. Transfer to small bowl. Cover with plastic wrap. Let sweat for about 15 minutes until cool enough to handle. Peel and discard skins. Cut into 1/3 inch (1 cm) slices. Put into large bowl.

Add next 5 ingredients. Toss.

Basil Dressing: Process all 7 ingredients in blender or food processor until smooth. Makes about 1/2 cup (125 mL) dressing. Drizzle over salad. Toss gently. Serves 10 to 12.

1 serving: 166 Calories; 9.8 g Total Fat (6.7 g Mono, 1 g Poly, 1.6 g Sat); 0 mg Cholesterol; 17 g Carbohydrate; 3 g Fibre; 4 g Protein; 269 mg Sodium

Pictured on front cover.

croutons

Trim the crusts from 4 white bread slices. Cut the bread into small cubes. Melt 2 tbsp. (30 mL) hard margarine (or butter) in a large frying pan on medium. Add the bread cubes. Cook for 3 to 4 minutes, stirring occasionally, until golden. Remove the croutons to a paper towel-lined plate. Cool.

tip

To easily cut bread slices into cubes, partially freeze the bread first. Trim the crusts and cube a stack of 5 to 6 bread slices at once.

This salad makes a great lunch or light supper. It's also a nice first course before grilled fish, pork or chicken. For extra crunch, add some chopped celery or sliced water chestnuts.

Apple And Shrimp Salad

Head of romaine lettuce, chopped or torn	1	1
Bags of frozen cooked medium shrimp (12 oz., 340 g, each), peeled and deveined, thawed	2	2
Tart medium cooking apples (such as Granny Smith), with peel and thinly sliced	2	2
Chopped walnuts	1/2 cup	125 mL
Raisins	1/2 cup	125 mL
CREAMY DILL DRESSING		
Mayonnaise (or salad dressing)	1/4 cup	60 mL
Sour cream	1/4 cup	60 mL
Olive (or cooking) oil	3 tbsp.	50 mL
White wine vinegar	2 tbsp.	30 mL
Chopped fresh dill (or 1 1/2 tsp., 7 mL, dill weed)	2 tbsp.	30 mL
Granulated sugar	2 tsp.	10 mL
Salt	3/4 tsp.	4 mL
Pepper	1/4 tsp.	1 mL

Put first 5 ingredients into large bowl. Toss.

Creamy Dill Dressing: Process all 8 ingredients in blender or food processor until smooth. Makes about 3/4 cup (175 mL) dressing. Drizzle over salad. Toss well. Serves 8.

1 serving: 305 Calories; 17.9 g Total Fat (8.6 g Mono, 6 g Poly, 2.5 g Sat); 173 mg Cholesterol; 16 g Carbohydrate; 2 g Fibre; 21 g Protein; 460 mg Sodium

Pictured on page 41.

A colourful, delicately flavoured salad with soft bites of Brie, tangy cranberries and crunchy croutons. A delightful first course for any meal.

Cranberry Brie Salad

Dried cranberries	1/2 cup	125 mL
Port wine	1/4 cup	60 mL
Head of butter lettuce, chopped or torn	1	1
Croutons	2/3 cup	150 mL
Brie cheese round, chopped	4 oz.	113 g

(continued on next page)

CRANBERRY DRESSING

Cranberry cocktail	2 tbsp.	30 mL
Olive (or cooking) oil	2 tbsp.	30 mL
Basil pesto	1 tbsp.	15 mL
Red wine vinegar	1 tbsp.	15 mL

Measure cranberries and wine into small bowl. Stir until coated. Let stand for 1 hour, stirring occasionally. Drain. Transfer cranberries to large bowl.

Add lettuce, croutons and cheese. Toss.

Cranberry Dressing: Combine all 4 ingredients in jar with tight-fitting lid. Shake well. Makes about 1/3 cup (75 mL) dressing. Drizzle over salad. Toss well. Serves 4.

1 serving: 245 Calories; 17.3 g Total Fat (8.8 g Mono, 1.1 g Poly, 6.4 g Sat); 28 mg Cholesterol; 14 g Carbohydrate; 3 g Fibre; 8 g Protein; 269 mg Sodium

Pictured below.

about cranberries

The cranberry is indigenous to North America and grows wild in several provinces. Native peoples of North America used cranberries for food and medicine, but the Pilgrims, legend has it, popularized them, serving them at the first Thanksgiving. Today, British Columbia produces the majority of cranberries grown commercially in Canada, followed by Quebec, Nova Scotia, Ontario and New Brunswick.

A colourful, hearty salad with a zesty lemon kick. Sweet honey and a hint of garlic are nicely balanced.

about arugula

Arugula resembles radish leaves and has a distinct peppery flavour. Often included in commercial mixed salad greens, it can also be found in bags or in bunches with the roots still attached. For optimum freshness, place the roots in a glass of water, cover with a plastic bag, and store in the refrigerator for up to 2 days. Alternatively, wrap the roots with damp paper towels and put in a plastic bag before refrigerating. Discard the roots and stems and wash the leaves thoroughly before using.

Warm Chicken Salad

Chopped fresh rosemary leaves (or 1/2 tsp., 2 mL, dried, crushed)	2 tsp.	10 mL
Olive (or cooking) oil	1 tsp.	5 mL
Grated lemon zest	1 tsp.	5 mL
Garlic clove, minced (or 1/4 tsp., 1 mL, powder)	1	1
Pepper	1/2 tsp.	2 mL
Boneless, skinless chicken breast halves	1/2 lb.	225 g
Prosciutto (or deli ham) slices, cooked crisp and crumbled	8	8
Can of chickpeas (garbanzo beans), rinsed and drained	19 oz.	540 mL
Thinly sliced English cucumber (with peel)	3/4 cup	175 mL
Bag of arugula (or mixed salad greens)	4 1/2 oz.	128 g
LEMON GARLIC DRESSING		
Olive (or cooking) oil	1/3 cup	75 mL
Lemon juice	1/4 cup	60 mL
Liquid honey	2 tbsp.	30 mL
Garlic clove, minced (or 1/4 tsp., 1 mL, powder)	1	1
Hot pepper sauce	1/2 tsp.	2 mL
Salt	1/4 tsp.	1 mL
Pepper	1/4 tsp.	1 mL

Combine first 5 ingredients in medium bowl. Add chicken. Turn until coated. Cover. Chill for 30 minutes. Preheat electric grill for 5 minutes or gas barbecue to medium (see Note). Cook chicken on greased grill for about 5 minutes per side until no longer pink inside. Transfer to large plate. Cut into 1/4 inch (6 mm) slices. Put into large bowl.

Add next 4 ingredients. Toss.

(continued on next page)

Lemon Garlic Dressing: Combine all 7 ingredients in jar with tight-fitting lid. Shake well. Makes about 3/4 cup (175 mL) dressing. Drizzle over salad. Toss well. Serve immediately. Serves 6.

1 serving: 307 Calories; 19.4 g Total Fat (12.3 g Mono, 2.2 g Poly, 3.6 g Sat); 29 mg Cholesterol; 19 g Carbohydrate; 2 g Fibre; 15 g Protein; 346 mg Sodium

Pictured below.

Note: Chicken may be broiled in the oven instead of grilled. Place chicken on a greased broiler pan. Broil on the top rack for about 5 minutes per side until no longer pink inside.

A classic salad that often pops up at potlucks! A great way to get the kids to eat their broccoli.

broccoli slaw

Instead of broccoli florets, use 4 cups (1 L) broccoli slaw, available in bags in the produce section of your grocery store.

Broccoli Salad

Broccoli florets	5 cups	1.25 L
Bacon slices, cooked crisp and crumbled	6	6
Diced red onion	1/2 cup	125 mL
Grated medium Cheddar cheese	1/2 cup	125 mL
Salted, roasted sunflower seeds (optional)	1/4 cup	60 mL
SWEET CREAMY DRESSING		
Light salad dressing (or light mayonnaise)	6 tbsp.	100 mL
Granulated sugar	2 tbsp.	30 mL
White vinegar	2 tbsp.	30 mL

Put first 5 ingredients into large bowl. Toss.

Sweet Creamy Dressing: Combine salad dressing, sugar and vinegar in small bowl. Makes about 1/2 cup (125 mL) dressing. Drizzle over salad. Toss well. Serves 6.

1 serving: 164 Calories; 10.5 g Total Fat (4.7 g Mono, 1.7 g Poly, 3.5 g Sat); 16 mg Cholesterol; 12 g Carbohydrate; 2 g Fibre; 7 g Protein; 299 mg Sodium

Pictured on page 49.

A good addition to a luncheon served on the patio. Garnish with slices of red pepper for an extra splash of colour.

variation

For an equally delicious salad, use 1/4 cup (60 mL) thinly sliced red onion instead of the green onions.

Bacon And Pea Salad

Bacon slices, cooked crisp and crumbled	5	5
Cold cooked peas	3 cups	750 mL
Light sour cream	1/3 cup	75 mL
Green onions, sliced	4	4
Chopped fresh dill (or 1/4 tsp., 1 mL, dill weed)	1 tsp.	5 mL
Salt	1/2 tsp.	2 mL
Pepper, sprinkle		

Combine all 7 ingredients in medium bowl. Serves 4.

1 serving: 164 Calories; 5.7 g Total Fat (2.7 g Mono, 0.7 g Poly, 3.2 g Sat); 11 mg Cholesterol; 19 g Carbohydrate; 6 g Fibre; 10 g Protein; 543 mg Sodium

Pictured on page 49.

Clockwise from top right:
Bacon And Pea Salad, above
Cheesy Pea Salad, page 50
Broccoli Salad, this page
Carrot Salad, page 50

A lovely salad to serve with grilled cheese sandwiches, hamburgers or hot dogs. Great for a picnic lunch, too!

Cheesy Pea Salad

Large hard-cooked eggs, chopped	3	3
Cold cooked peas	2 cups	500 mL
Thinly sliced celery	1 cup	250 mL
Diced light sharp Cheddar cheese	1/2 cup	125 mL
Sweet pickle relish	1/3 cup	75 mL
Salt, sprinkle		
Pepper, sprinkle		
CREAMY DRESSING		
Light salad dressing (or light mayonnaise)	1/4 cup	60 mL
Milk	1 1/2 tbsp.	25 mL
Granulated sugar	1/4 tsp.	1 mL

Combine first 7 ingredients in medium bowl.

Creamy Dressing: Combine salad dressing, milk and sugar in small bowl. Makes about 1/4 cup (60 mL) dressing. Drizzle over salad. Toss well. Serves 6.

1 serving: 177 Calories; 8.9 g Total Fat (3.6 g Mono, 1.3 g Poly, 3.1 g Sat); 118 mg Cholesterol; 16 g Carbohydrate; 3 g Fibre; 9 g Protein; 358 mg Sodium

Pictured on page 49.

Colourful carrot salad accented with sweet raisins. This is a delicious classic, enjoyed by many throughout the years.

cranberry carrot salad

Instead of raisins, use the same amount of dried cranberries for a tangy burst of flavour.

Carrot Salad

Grated carrot	3 cups	750 mL
Chopped celery	1/2 cup	125 mL
Raisins	1/2 cup	125 mL
CREAMY MUSTARD DRESSING		
Salad dressing (or mayonnaise)	1/2 cup	125 mL
White vinegar	1 tbsp.	15 mL
Granulated sugar	1 1/2 tsp.	7 mL
Prepared mustard	1/4 tsp.	1 mL
Paprika	1/8 tsp.	0.5 mL

(continued on next page)

Put carrot, celery and raisins into medium bowl. Toss.

Creamy Mustard Dressing: Combine all 5 ingredients in small bowl. Makes about 1/4 cup (60 mL) dressing. Drizzle over salad. Toss well. Serves 4.

1 serving: 258 Calories; 15.5 g Total Fat (8.4 g Mono, 5.2 g Poly, 1.2 g Sat); 8 mg Cholesterol; 30 g Carbohydrate; 3 g Fibre; 2 g Protein; 246 mg Sodium

Pictured on page 49.

Vegetable Marinade

Small head of cauliflower, separated into florets	1	1
Broccoli florets	3 cups	750 mL
Cherry tomatoes	2 cups	500 mL
Celery ribs, cut into 1 inch (2.5 cm) pieces	3	3
Medium carrots, cut into 1 inch (2.5 cm) pieces	3	3
Fresh whole white mushrooms (or two 10 oz., 284 mL, cans of whole mushrooms, drained)	2 cups	500 mL
Green medium pepper, cut into strips or rings	1	1
Italian dressing	1 cup	250 mL

Put first 7 ingredients into large bowl. Toss.

Drizzle dressing over vegetables. Toss until coated. Cover. Chill for at least 6 hours or overnight, tossing occasionally. Drain. Serves 12.

1 serving: 172 Calories; 14.7 g Total Fat (8 g Mono, 4.9 g Poly, 1.1 g Sat); 14 mg Cholesterol; 10 g Carbohydrate; 3 g Fibre; 3 g Protein; 377 mg Sodium

So simple to make and so delicious! Mix and match your favourite fresh vegetables according to your family's tastes. Toss veggies with our Italian Dressing, page 104, for an extra-fresh flavour.

variation

Instead of using Italian dressing, toss the vegetables with the same amount of Ginger Dressing or Sesame Soy Dressing, page 112, for a tasty change of pace.

A delicious salad that's always a hit. Makes lots, so it's a great potluck choice as well.

tip

To toast almonds and sesame seeds, spread them in a single layer in separate ungreased shallow pans. Bake in a 350°F (175°C) oven for 5 to 10 minutes, stirring or shaking often, until desired doneness.

japanese shrimp salad

Add 2 cups (500 mL) cooked small shrimp (peeled and deveined), and 1/2 cup (125 mL) each of sliced English cucumber (with peel) and sliced radish before tossing salad with dressing.

oriental chicken salad

Add 2 cups (500 mL) chopped cooked chicken, and 1/2 cup (125 mL) each of sliced English cucumber (with peel) and sliced radish before tossing salad with dressing.

Japanese Cabbage Salad

Medium head of cabbage, shredded	1/2	1/2
Fresh bean sprouts	4 1/2 cups	1.1 L
Sliced fresh white mushrooms	2 cups	500 mL
Sliced or slivered almonds, toasted (see Tip)	1/2 cup	125 mL
Raw sunflower seeds	1/4 cup	60 mL
Sesame seeds, toasted (see Tip)	2 tbsp.	30 mL
Green onions, chopped	2	2
ASIAN DRESSING		
Seasoning packet from instant noodles		
Cooking (or olive) oil	1/2 cup	125 mL
White vinegar	3 tbsp.	50 mL
Soy sauce	2 – 4 tbsp.	30 – 60 mL
Granulated sugar	1 tbsp.	15 mL
Salt	1 tsp.	5 mL
Pepper	1/2 tsp.	2 mL
Package of instant noodles with chicken-flavoured seasoning packet	3 oz.	85 g
Dry chow mein noodles	1 1/2 cups	375 mL

Put first 7 ingredients into large bowl. Toss.

Asian Dressing: Empty seasoning packet into jar with tight-fitting lid. Add next 6 ingredients. Shake well. Makes about 3/4 cup (175 mL) dressing. Drizzle over salad. Toss well.

Just before serving, break up instant noodles. Scatter over top. Sprinkle with chow mein noodles. Serves 10 to 12.

1 serving: 297 Calories; 23.2 g Total Fat (11.1 g Mono, 8.7 g Poly, 2.2 g Sat); 0 mg Cholesterol; 20 g Carbohydrate; 3 g Fibre; 6 g Protein; 593 mg Sodium

Pictured on page 53.

Serve this delicious side salad with barbecued ribs or pork chops. Store in the refrigerator for up to 2 days.

time saver

Make this coleslaw more quickly by using a package of coleslaw mix, available in the produce section of your grocery store.

Creamy Celery Seed Slaw

Shredded green cabbage, lightly packed	3 cups	750 mL
Shredded red cabbage, lightly packed	2 cups	500 mL
Grated carrot	3/4 cup	175 mL
Thinly sliced green onion	1/4 cup	60 mL
CELERY SEED DRESSING		
Mayonnaise (or salad dressing)	1 cup	250 mL
Apple cider vinegar	2 tbsp.	30 mL
Granulated sugar	2 tbsp.	30 mL
Chopped fresh parsley (or 3/4 tsp., 4 mL, flakes)	1 tbsp.	15 mL
Celery seed	1 1/2 tsp.	7 mL
Salt	1/4 tsp.	1 mL

Put first 4 ingredients into large bowl. Toss.

Celery Seed Dressing: Combine all 6 ingredients in small bowl. Makes about 1 1/4 cups (300 mL) dressing. Drizzle over cabbage mixture. Toss well. Chill for 1 hour to blend flavours. Serves 6.

1 serving: 326 Calories; 31.5 g Total Fat (17.4 g Mono, 10.5 g Poly, 3 g Sat); 23 mg Cholesterol; 11 g Carbohydrate; 2 g Fibre; 2 g Protein; 316 mg Sodium

Pictured on page 55.

A crisp, sweet slaw. Sure to become a favourite. Keeps in the refrigerator for up to a week.

Overnight Coleslaw

Medium head of cabbage, shredded	1	1
Medium onion, thinly sliced	1	1
Green medium pepper, cut into short thin strips	1	1
White vinegar	1 cup	250 mL
Cooking (or olive) oil	2/3 cup	150 mL
Granulated sugar	1/2 cup	125 mL
Prepared mustard	2 tsp.	10 mL
Celery seed	1 tsp.	5 mL
Salt	1 tsp.	5 mL
Pepper	1/4 tsp.	1 mL

(continued on next page)

Put cabbage, onion and green pepper into large bowl. Toss.

Measure remaining 7 ingredients into medium saucepan. Heat on medium-high, stirring occasionally, until boiling. Boil for 1 minute. Drizzle over vegetables. Stir well. Press vegetables with spoon into vinegar mixture. Cover. Chill for at least 6 hours or overnight to blend flavours. Serves 10.

1 serving: 213 Calories; 15.8 g Total Fat (9.1 g Mono, 4.8 g Poly, 1.2 g Sat); 0 mg Cholesterol; 19 g Carbohydrate; 2 g Fibre; 2 g Protein; 271 mg Sodium

Pictured below.

Left: Creamy Celery Seed Slaw, page 54
Right: Overnight Coleslaw, page 54

A unique salad combination. Increase the amount of chili paste if you'd like a little more heat.

tip

To toast cashews, spread them in a single layer in an ungreased shallow pan. Bake in a 350°F (175°C) oven for 5 to 10 minutes, stirring or shaking often, until desired doneness.

about blanching

Salad recipes call for blanching to brighten the colour of fresh vegetables and help maintain their crispness. To blanch vegetables, immerse small batches briefly in boiling water (photo 1), then immediately plunge them into ice water to stop the cooking process. Leave vegetables in the water until cold, changing the water if it warms (photo 2).

Blanching times vary, from 30 seconds to 5 or more minutes, depending on the vegetable. Start timing once the water is boiling again. Be sure to follow your recipe carefully so that vegetables are blanched, and not cooked through.

Bean And Cashew Salad

Fresh whole green beans	1/2 lb.	225 g
Boiling water		
Ice water		
Halved cherry tomatoes	2 cups	500 mL
Plain cashews, toasted (see Tip)	1 cup	250 mL
Thinly sliced red onion	3/4 cup	175 mL
LEMON DILL DRESSING		
Olive (or cooking) oil	1/3 cup	75 mL
Lemon juice	3 tbsp.	50 mL
Chopped fresh dill (or 1/2 tsp., 2 mL, dill weed)	2 tsp.	10 mL
Garlic clove, minced (or 1/4 tsp., 1 mL, powder)	1	1
Chili paste (sambal oelek)	1/2 tsp.	2 mL
Salt	1/4 tsp.	1 mL

Blanch beans in boiling water in large saucepan for 1 to 3 minutes until bright green. Drain. Immediately plunge into ice water in large bowl. Let stand for about 10 minutes until cold. Drain. Transfer to separate large bowl.

Add tomato, cashews and onion. Toss.

Lemon Dill Dressing: Combine all 6 ingredients in jar with tight-fitting lid. Shake well. Makes about 1/2 cup (125 mL) dressing. Drizzle over salad. Toss well. Serves 8.

1 serving: 211 Calories; 18 g Total Fat (11.9 g Mono, 2.3 g Poly, 3 g Sat); 0 mg Cholesterol; 11 g Carbohydrate; 1 g Fibre; 4 g Protein; 82 mg Sodium

Pictured on page 57.

Use a slotted spoon to serve this colourful, tasty salad. Double the onion rings if you like more. Makes lots—a real crowd pleaser!

tip

Rinsing and draining canned beans removes much of the sodium used in the canning process. It also enhances their appearance for use in salads by removing the canning liquid. In marinated salads, the liquid from canned beans may be used to contribute extra flavour to the marinade.

Bean Salad

Can of cut green beans (do not drain)	14 oz.	398 mL
Can of cut yellow wax beans, rinsed and drained	14 oz.	398 mL
Can of lima beans, rinsed and drained	14 oz.	398 mL
Can of kidney beans, rinsed and drained	14 oz.	398 mL
Small onion, sliced and separated into rings	1	1
Sliced celery	1 cup	250 mL
Jar of pimiento, well drained and chopped	2 oz.	57 mL
Granulated sugar	1 cup	250 mL
Dry mustard	1/2 tsp.	2 mL
Salt	1/4 tsp.	1 mL
White vinegar	1 cup	250 mL
Cooking (or olive) oil	2 tbsp.	30 mL

Put green beans with liquid into large bowl. Add next 6 ingredients. Stir.

Combine sugar, mustard and salt in small bowl. Add vinegar and cooking oil. Stir until sugar is dissolved. Drizzle over salad. Stir. Cover. Chill for 24 hours to blend flavours. Store in refrigerator for up to 3 weeks. Serves 16.

1 serving: 72 Calories; 1.2 g Total Fat (0.7 g Mono, 0.4 g Poly, 0.1 g Sat); 0 mg Cholesterol; 14 g Carbohydrate; 1 g Fibre; 2 g Protein; 107 mg Sodium

Pictured on page 59.

An easy salad. Cool and refreshing.

variation

For a sweet, tangy dressing, add 2 tbsp. (30 mL) each of lemon juice, chopped fresh parsley and granulated sugar to the sour cream mixture.

Cucumbers In Sour Cream

English cucumbers (with peel)	3	3
Salt	1 1/2 tsp.	7 mL
Sour cream	1 cup	250 mL
Chopped fresh dill (or 1/2 tsp., 2 mL, dill weed)	2 tsp.	10 mL

Score cucumbers (see Note). Thinly slice. Put into large bowl. Sprinkle with salt. Stir. Cover. Chill for 1 hour. Drain.

(continued on next page)

Combine sour cream and dill in small bowl. Add to cucumber. Stir until coated. Serves 12.

1 serving: 42 Calories; 3 g Total Fat (0.8 g Mono, 0.2 g Poly, 1.8 g Sat); 8 mg Cholesterol; 3 g Carbohydrate; 1 g Fibre; 1 g Protein; 159 mg Sodium

Pictured below.

Note: To score a cucumber, drag a fork or a zesting tool lengthwise down the peel, using an even pressure. Repeat all around the cucumber to create a pretty green and white striped effect.

Left: Cucumbers In Sour Cream, page 58
Right: Bean Salad, page 58

You won't be able to stop eating these once you start! They have a great sweet and sour flavour.

Crispy Cukes

White vinegar	1 cup	250 mL
Granulated sugar	1 cup	250 mL
Water	1 cup	250 mL
Salt	1 tbsp.	15 mL
Pepper	1/4 tsp.	1 mL
Onion powder	1/4 tsp.	1 mL
English cucumbers (with peel)	4	4

Measure first 6 ingredients into large bowl. Stir until sugar is dissolved.

Score cucumbers (see Note). Cut into thin slices. Add to vinegar mixture. Stir. Cover. Chill for 24 hours to blend flavours. Store in refrigerator for up to 1 week. Serves 8.

1 serving: 129 Calories; 0.2 g Total Fat (0 g Mono, 0.1 g Poly, 0.1 g Sat); 0 mg Cholesterol; 33 g Carbohydrate; 1 g Fibre; 1 g Protein; 888 mg Sodium

Pictured on page 63.

Note: To score a cucumber, drag a fork or a zesting tool lengthwise down the peel, using an even pressure. Repeat all around the cucumber to create a pretty green and white striped effect.

Chickpeas pack this delicious, crunchy salad with protein. A great choice for lunch! This salad may be stored in the refrigerator for up to 3 days.

Chickpea Tomato Salad

Can of chickpeas (garbanzo beans), rinsed and drained	19 oz.	540 mL
Can of stewed tomatoes, drained and chopped	14 oz.	398 mL
Thinly sliced celery	1/2 cup	125 mL
Diced red pepper	1/2 cup	125 mL
Green onion, thinly sliced	1	1

(continued on next page)

BASIL MUSTARD DRESSING

Olive (or cooking) oil	2 tbsp.	30 mL
White vinegar	2 tbsp.	30 mL
Chopped fresh parsley (or 2 tsp., 10 mL, flakes)	2 1/2 tbsp.	37 mL
Chopped fresh basil (or 1/2 tsp., 2 mL, dried)	2 tsp.	10 mL
Dry mustard	1/4 tsp.	1 mL
Garlic powder	1/8 tsp.	0.5 mL

tip

For easier preparation, make marinated salads in bowls or other containers with tight-fitting lids. Turn the container over occasionally, instead of stirring the salad, to distribute the marinade evenly.

Put first 5 ingredients into medium bowl. Stir.

Basil Mustard Dressing: Combine all 6 ingredients in small bowl. Makes about 1/4 cup (60 mL) dressing. Drizzle over salad. Stir. Cover. Chill for at least 6 hours or overnight, stirring occasionally. Serves 6.

1 serving: 131 Calories; 5.8 g Total Fat (3.6 g Mono, 0.9 g Poly, 0.8 g Sat); 0 mg Cholesterol; 17 g Carbohydrate; 3 g Fibre; 4 g Protein; 288 mg Sodium

Pictured below.

A wonderful combination of fresh tastes in a colourful, summery salad.

tip

To toast pecans, spread them in a single layer in an ungreased shallow pan. Bake in a 350°F (175°C) oven for 5 to 10 minutes, stirring or shaking often, until desired doneness.

storing tomatoes

To maintain optimum flavour, store tomatoes at room temperature. Refrigeration will stop the ripening process and alter a tomato's flavour and texture.

Tomato Pineapple Salad

Roma (plum) tomatoes, quartered lengthwise	6	6
Can of pineapple tidbits, drained	14 oz.	398 mL
Thinly sliced red onion	1/4 cup	60 mL
Coarsely chopped fresh basil (or 1 1/2 tsp., 7 mL, dried)	2 tbsp.	30 mL
CHILI GARLIC DRESSING		
Olive (or cooking) oil	2 tbsp.	30 mL
White (or red) wine vinegar	2 tbsp.	30 mL
Garlic clove, minced (or 1/4 tsp., 1 mL, powder)	1	1
Dried crushed chilies	1/4 tsp.	1 mL
Salt	1/4 tsp.	1 mL
Pepper	1/4 tsp.	1 mL
Coarsely chopped pecans, toasted (see Tip)	1/3 cup	75 mL

Put first 4 ingredients into medium bowl. Toss gently.

Chili Garlic Dressing: Combine first 6 ingredients in jar with tight-fitting lid. Shake well. Makes about 1/4 cup (60 mL) dressing. Drizzle over salad. Toss gently.

Sprinkle with pecans. Serves 6.

1 serving: 139 Calories; 9.8 g Total Fat (5.7 g Mono, 2.7 g Poly, 0.8 g Sat); 0 mg Cholesterol; 14 g Carbohydrate; 3 g Fibre; 2 g Protein; 112 mg Sodium

Pictured on page 63.

Clockwise from top right:
Creamy Corn Salad, page 64
Tomato Pineapple Salad, above
Beet Salad, page 66
Crispy Cukes, page 60

A salad you just have to try! Deliciously spiced and bursting with colour.

storing garlic

Fresh garlic should be stored at room temperature in a cool, dry place. Refrigeration will dehydrate the cloves, affecting the garlic's flavour, and may result in other refrigerated foods absorbing its odour.

Creamy Corn Salad

Can of black beans, rinsed and drained	14 oz.	398 mL
Can of kernel corn, drained	12 oz.	341 mL
Medium tomatoes, seeds removed, finely chopped	2	2
Finely chopped red onion	1/2 cup	125 mL
Finely chopped red pepper	1/2 cup	125 mL
Chopped fresh cilantro or parsley (optional)	2 tbsp.	30 mL

SPICY RANCH DRESSING

Ranch dressing	1/4 cup	60 mL
Lime juice	1 tbsp.	15 mL
Ground cumin	1/4 tsp.	1 mL
Chili powder	1/4 tsp.	1 mL
Garlic clove, minced (or 1/4 tsp., 1 mL, powder)	1	1
Salt	1/4 tsp.	1 mL

Put first 6 ingredients into large bowl. Toss.

Spicy Ranch Dressing: Combine all 6 ingredients in small bowl. Makes about 2/3 cup (150 mL) dressing. Drizzle over salad. Toss well. Serves 6.

1 serving: 150 Calories; 4.6 g Total Fat (2.3 g Mono, 1.6 g Poly, 0.4 g Sat); 3 mg Cholesterol; 24 g Carbohydrate; 4 g Fibre; 5 g Protein; 395 mg Sodium

Pictured on page 63.

This unique combination of nippy radishes, sweet oranges and spices is certain to enliven dinner.

Radish And Orange Salad

Thinly sliced radish	3 cups	750 mL
Can of mandarin orange segments, drained	10 oz.	284 mL
Slivered almonds, toasted (see Tip)	1/3 cup	75 mL
Sliced green onion	1/4 cup	60 mL
Dried crushed chilies	3/4 – 1 tsp.	4 – 5 mL

(continued on next page)

CHILI BASIL DRESSING

Olive (or cooking) oil	3 tbsp.	50 mL
White wine vinegar	2 tbsp.	30 mL
Chopped fresh basil (or 3/4 tsp., 4 mL, dried)	1 tbsp.	15 mL
Chili powder	1/4 tsp.	1 mL
Ground coriander	1/8 tsp.	0.5 mL
Salt	1/8 tsp.	0.5 mL
Pepper	1/8 tsp.	0.5 mL

tip

To toast almonds, spread them in a single layer in an ungreased shallow pan. Bake in a 350°F (175°C) oven for 5 to 10 minutes, stirring or shaking often, until desired doneness.

Put first 5 ingredients into medium bowl. Toss gently.

Chili Basil Dressing: Combine all 7 ingredients in jar with tight-fitting lid. Shake well. Makes about 1/3 cup (75 mL) dressing. Drizzle over salad. Toss gently. Serves 4.

1 serving: 198 Calories; 16.9 g Total Fat (11.5 g Mono, 2.2 g Poly, 2 g Sat); 0 mg Cholesterol; 12 g Carbohydrate; 3 g Fibre; 3 g Protein; 109 mg Sodium

Pictured below.

Beet Salad

Brightly coloured and crunchy good! A savoury twist on a Waldorf salad.

Cans of sliced beets (14 oz., 398 mL, each), drained and diced	2	2
Sliced celery	1 cup	250 mL
Medium apple, peeled and diced	1	1
Chopped walnuts	1/4 cup	60 mL
Salt	1/2 tsp.	2 mL
CREAMY HORSERADISH DRESSING		
Sour cream	1/4 cup	60 mL
Mayonnaise (or salad dressing)	1/4 cup	60 mL
Prepared horseradish	1/2 tsp.	2 mL

Combine first 5 ingredients in large bowl.

Creamy Horseradish Dressing: Combine sour cream, mayonnaise and horseradish in small bowl. Makes about 1/2 cup (125 mL) dressing. Drizzle over salad. Toss gently. Serves 8.

1 serving: 119 Calories; 9.5 g Total Fat (4.1 g Mono, 3.6 g Poly, 1.4 g Sat); 7 mg Cholesterol; 8 g Carbohydrate; 2 g Fibre; 2 g Protein; 351 mg Sodium

Pictured on page 63.

Bean Sprout Salad

This not-so-common salad is excellent. Try it for a change from the ordinary.

Snow peas, trimmed	6 oz.	170 g
Boiling water		
Ice water		
Fresh bean sprouts	4 1/2 cups	1.1 L
Shredded cabbage, lightly packed	1 cup	250 mL
Chopped pimiento	2 tbsp.	30 mL
SOY DRESSING		
Olive (or cooking) oil	2 tbsp.	30 mL
Soy sauce	2 tbsp.	30 mL
White vinegar	2 tbsp.	30 mL
Brown sugar, packed	2 tbsp.	30 mL

(continued on next page)

Blanch snow peas in boiling water in medium saucepan for about 1 minute until bright green. Drain. Immediately plunge into ice water in large bowl. Let stand for about 10 minutes until cold. Drain. Transfer to separate large bowl.

Add bean sprouts, cabbage and pimiento. Toss.

Soy Dressing: Combine all 4 ingredients in small bowl. Makes about 1/3 cup (75 mL) dressing. Drizzle over salad. Toss well. Serves 6.

1 serving: *97 Calories; 4.9 g Total Fat (2.7 g Mono, 1.5 g Poly, 0.4 g Sat); 0 mg Cholesterol; 12 g Carbohydrate; 2 g Fibre; 4 g Protein; 358 mg Sodium*

Pictured below.

Three fruits mingle in a tasty jellied salad. Excellent with roast turkey or chicken.

tip

To successfully unmold a gelatin salad, first make sure it is completely set. Gently loosen the gelatin from the edge of the mold or pan using damp fingers or a spatula dipped in warm water. Dip the mold into warm (not hot) water for about 15 seconds. Place a serving plate on top of the mold and invert both the mold and plate. Shake slightly to loosen. Carefully remove the mold. If the gelatin does not release easily, dip the mold into warm water again for a few seconds.

Cranberry Jelly Salad

Box of cherry-flavoured jelly powder (gelatin)	3 oz.	85 g
Envelope of unflavoured gelatin (about 1 tbsp., 15 mL)	1/4 oz.	7 g
Boiling water	1 1/4 cups	300 mL
Can of crushed pineapple (with juice)	14 oz.	398 mL
Can of whole cranberry sauce	14 oz.	398 mL
Finely diced red apple (with peel)	1/2 cup	125 mL

Combine jelly powder and gelatin in medium bowl. Add boiling water. Stir until dissolved.

Add pineapple with juice, cranberry sauce and apple. Stir. Chill, stirring occasionally, until slightly thickened. Pour into lightly greased 4 1/2 to 5 cup (1.1 to 1.25 L) mold. Chill for 2 to 3 hours until set. Serves 8.

1 serving: 167 Calories; 0.2 g Total Fat (0 g Mono, 0 g Poly, 0 g Sat); 0 mg Cholesterol; 42 g Carbohydrate; 1 g Fibre; 2 g Protein; 46 mg Sodium

Pictured on page 69.

Clockwise from top left:
Apricot Salad, page 70
Apricot Sauce, page 70
Cranberry Jelly Salad, above
Cherry Cheese Salad, page 71

A beautiful salad and a heavenly sauce! Garnish with canned apricot halves for a fabulous finishing touch.

pretty presentation

Instead of using a mold, pour the salad mixture into a lightly greased 9 x 9 inch (22 x 22 cm) pan. Chill until set. Cut into squares and spoon the sauce over individual servings.

Apricot Salad

Boxes of orange-flavoured jelly powder (gelatin), 3 oz. (85 g), each	2	2
Boiling water	1 1/2 cups	375 mL
Jars of strained apricot baby food (4 1/2 oz., 128 mL, each)	2	2
Can of crushed pineapple (with juice)	14 oz.	398 mL
APRICOT SAUCE		
Granulated sugar	1/2 cup	125 mL
All-purpose flour	3 tbsp.	50 mL
Jar of strained apricot baby food	4 1/2 oz.	128 mL
Pineapple juice	1/2 cup	125 mL
Whipping cream (see Note)	1 cup	250 mL
Grated medium Cheddar cheese	1 cup	250 mL

Empty jelly powder into large bowl. Add boiling water. Stir until dissolved.

Add strained apricot and pineapple with juice. Stir. Chill, stirring often, until starting to thicken. Pour into lightly greased 4 1/2 cup (1.1 L) mold. Chill until set.

Apricot Sauce: Combine sugar and flour in small saucepan.

Add strained apricot and pineapple juice. Heat and stir on medium for about 5 minutes until boiling and thickened. Cool. Transfer to medium bowl. Chill.

Beat whipping cream in small bowl until stiff peaks form. Fold about 1/3 of whipped cream into apricot mixture to lighten. Fold in remaining whipped cream and cheese. Makes about 3 cups (750 mL) sauce. Serve with salad. Serves 8.

1 serving: 453 Calories; 15.2 g Total Fat (4.4 g Mono, 0.5 g Poly, 9.5 g Sat); 52 mg Cholesterol; 77 g Carbohydrate; 1 g Fibre; 7 g Protein; 181 mg Sodium

Pictured on page 69.

Note: If preferred, use 1 envelope of dessert topping (prepared) instead of the whipping cream. This salad will be a bit sweeter, but still very good.

Cherry Cheese Salad

Box of raspberry-flavoured jelly powder (gelatin)	3 oz.	85 g
Boiling water	1 cup	250 mL
Can of cherry pie filling	19 oz.	540 mL
Box of lemon-flavoured jelly powder (gelatin)	3 oz.	85 g
Boiling water	1 cup	250 mL
Block of cream cheese, softened	4 oz.	125 g
Salad dressing (or mayonnaise)	1/3 cup	75 mL
Crushed pineapple (with juice)	1 cup	250 mL
Whipping cream (see Note)	1 cup	250 mL
Miniature marshmallows	1 1/2 cups	375 mL
Chopped walnuts	2 tbsp.	30 mL
Green leaf lettuce leaves	9	9

Empty raspberry jelly powder into large bowl. Add first amount of boiling water. Stir until dissolved. Add pie filling. Stir. Spread evenly in lightly greased 9 x 9 inch (22 x 22 cm) pan. Chill until almost set.

Empty lemon jelly powder into small bowl. Add second amount of boiling water. Stir until dissolved.

Beat cream cheese and salad dressing in separate large bowl until smooth. Add lemon jelly powder mixture and pineapple with juice. Stir well. Chill until slightly thickened.

Beat whipping cream in medium bowl until stiff peaks form. Fold into cream cheese mixture. Fold in marshmallows. Spread on top of cherry layer in pan.

Sprinkle with walnuts. Chill until set. Cut into 9 pieces. Serve on lettuce leaves on individual salad plates. Serves 9.

1 serving: 382 Calories; 19.5 g Total Fat (6.8 g Mono, 2.7 g Poly, 9.1 g Sat); 50 mg Cholesterol; 51 g Carbohydrate; 1 g Fibre; 4 g Protein; 167 mg Sodium

Pictured on page 69.

Note: If preferred, use 1 envelope of dessert topping (prepared) instead of the whipping cream. This salad will be a bit sweeter, but still very good.

This colourful, creamy salad is just right for a bridal shower or a club get-together.

another pretty presentation

Instead of cutting into individual pieces, invert the entire salad onto a lettuce-lined serving platter. To loosen, place a warm, damp tea towel on the bottom of the pan. Gently shake the pan and platter until the salad releases. Beautiful for a buffet!

This refreshing salad goes well with just about anything.

perfect cucumber salad

Omit the sour cream. Pour the entire amount of slightly thickened cucumber mixture into the mold. Chill until set. Makes a sparkling clear salad.

cucumber sour cream salad

Increase the sour cream to 1 cup (250 mL). Add to the entire amount of slightly thickened cucumber mixture. Stir. Pour into the mold. Chill until set. Makes a completely different salad—creamy and soft.

A tropical delight! The presentation of this refreshing, healthy fruit salad is perfect for a buffet luncheon.

Layered Cucumber Salad

Box of lime-flavoured jelly powder (gelatin)	3 oz.	85 g
Boiling water	1/2 cup	125 mL
Finely grated English cucumber (with peel)	1 cup	250 mL
Finely chopped onion (or 1 tbsp., 15 mL, onion flakes)	1/4 cup	60 mL
Lemon juice	2 tbsp.	30 mL
Salt	1/4 tsp.	1 mL
Sour cream	1/2 cup	125 mL

Empty jelly powder into large bowl. Add boiling water. Stir until dissolved.

Add next 4 ingredients. Stir. Chill, stirring occasionally, until slightly thickened. Spoon 1/2 of cucumber mixture into lightly greased 3 cup (750 mL) mold. Chill until almost set. Chill remaining cucumber mixture in bowl until almost set.

Add sour cream to cucumber mixture in bowl. Stir. Spread over layer in mold. Chill until set. Serves 6.

1 serving: 91 Calories; 2.9 g Total Fat (0.8 g Mono, 0.1 g Poly, 1.8 g Sat); 8 mg Cholesterol; 15 g Carbohydrate; trace Fibre; 2 g Protein; 144 mg Sodium

Pineapple Boat Salad

Fresh pineapple (with leaves attached), halved lengthwise	1	1
Halved fresh strawberries	1 cup	250 mL
Halved seedless green (or red) grapes	1/2 cup	125 mL
Kiwifruit, sliced	1	1
Medium banana, sliced	1	1
1% cottage cheese	1 cup	250 mL
Chopped pecans (or walnuts)	1/4 cup	60 mL
Chopped green onion	1 tbsp.	15 mL
Chopped pecans (or walnuts), for garnish		

(continued on next page)

Remove and discard core from each pineapple half. Cut out pineapple, leaving 1/2 inch (12 mm) shell. Cut pineapple into bite-size pieces. Put into medium bowl.

Add next 4 ingredients. Toss gently. Spoon into each pineapple half.

Combine cottage cheese, first amount of pecans and green onion. Spoon on top of fruit mixture.

Garnish with second amount of pecans. Serves 4.

1 serving: 221 Calories; 6.9 g Total Fat (3.6 g Mono, 1.6 g Poly, 0.9 g Sat); 3 mg Cholesterol; 34 g Carbohydrate; 4 g Fibre; 10 g Protein; 253 mg Sodium

Pictured below.

One, two, three and you're done! A not-too-sweet salad that will leave them wanting more.

Quick Fruit Salad

Miniature marshmallows	2 1/2 cups	625 mL
Can of fruit cocktail, drained	14 oz.	398 mL
Sour cream	1 cup	250 mL
Chopped walnuts	1/4 cup	60 mL
Lettuce leaves	4	4
Maraschino cherries	4	4

Combine first 4 ingredients in large bowl. Chill for at least 1 hour.

Arrange lettuce leaves on 4 salad plates. Spoon fruit cocktail mixture on top of each.

Top each with 1 cherry. Serves 4.

1 serving: 273 Calories; 13.4 g Total Fat (3.5 g Mono, 3.5 g Poly, 5.6 g Sat); 24 mg Cholesterol; 37 g Carbohydrate; 1 g Fibre; 5 g Protein; 45 mg Sodium

Pictured on page 77.

An old familiar favourite. Just as good as it's always been!

Old-Fashioned Waldorf

Diced peeled apple	1 cup	250 mL
Chopped celery	1 cup	250 mL
Halved seedless red grapes	1/2 cup	125 mL
Chopped walnuts	1/2 cup	125 mL
Whipping cream (see Note)	1 cup	250 mL
Granulated sugar	1/4 cup	60 mL
White vinegar	3 tbsp.	50 mL

Combine first 4 ingredients in medium bowl.

Beat whipping cream in small bowl until soft peaks form. Add sugar. Beat just until stiff peaks form. Add vinegar. Stir. Add to apple mixture. Fold gently. Serves 4.

1 serving: 380 Calories; 29.8 g Total Fat (8 g Mono, 6.9 g Poly, 13.3 g Sat); 73 mg Cholesterol; 27 g Carbohydrate; 2 g Fibre; 6 g Protein; 51 mg Sodium

Note: For equally good results, omit the whipping cream and granulated sugar and use 1 envelope of dessert topping, prepared.

Pistachio Salad

Box of instant pistachio pudding powder (4 serving size)	1	1
Milk	1 3/4 cups	425 mL
Miniature marshmallows	2 cups	500 mL
Can of crushed pineapple, drained	14 oz.	398 mL
Chopped walnuts (optional)	1/2 cup	125 mL
Whipping cream (see Note)	1 cup	250 mL
Lettuce leaves (or shredded lettuce)	8 – 10	8 – 10

Empty pudding powder into medium bowl. Add milk. Stir until smooth.

Add marshmallows, pineapple and walnuts. Stir.

Beat whipping cream in small bowl until stiff peaks form. Fold into pudding mixture. Chill. Serve on lettuce leaves on individual salad plates. Serves 8 to 10.

1 serving: 224 Calories; 10.9 g Total Fat (3.2 g Mono, 0.4 g Poly, 6.7 g Sat); 39 mg Cholesterol; 30 g Carbohydrate; trace Fibre; 3 g Protein; 231 mg Sodium

Note: If preferred, use 1 envelope of dessert topping (prepared) instead of the whipping cream. This salad will be a bit sweeter, but still very good.

Such a treat to eat, and so different. Good right out of the bowl or spooned over fresh fruit.

variation

For a more solid, less creamy salad, omit the milk and use the same amount of pineapple juice.

Rum and coconut add a tropical flair to this attractive salad. For those with a sweet tooth, more sugar may be added.

tip

To toast coconut, spread in a single layer in an ungreased shallow pan. Bake in a 350°F (175°C) oven for 5 to 10 minutes, stirring or shaking often, until desired doneness.

Rum Fruit Salad

Lime juice	1/3 cup	75 mL
Granulated sugar	1/3 cup	75 mL
Dark (navy) rum	1/4 cup	60 mL
Cubed papaya	2 cups	500 mL
Cubed fresh pineapple (or two 14 oz., 398 mL, cans of pineapple tidbits, drained)	2 cups	500 mL
Large oranges, peeled and segmented	4	4
Flake coconut, toasted (see Tip)	3 tbsp.	50 mL

Combine lime juice and sugar in small saucepan. Heat and stir on low for about 5 minutes until sugar is dissolved. Bring to a boil on medium-high. Boil gently, uncovered, for 3 to 5 minutes, stirring occasionally, until slightly thickened.

Add rum. Stir. Cool.

Put papaya, pineapple and orange segments into large bowl. Drizzle with rum mixture. Stir until coated. Chill for 3 hours, stirring occasionally.

Sprinkle with coconut. Serves 6.

1 serving: *186 Calories; 2.3 g Total Fat (0.2 g Mono, 0.2 g Poly, 1.7 g Sat); 0 mg Cholesterol; 38 g Carbohydrate; 4 g Fibre; 2 g Protein; 3 mg Sodium*

Pictured on page 77.

Clockwise from top left:
Rum Fruit Salad, above
Apricot Dressing, page 78
Fresh Fruit Salad, page 78
Quick Fruit Salad, page 74

A festive presentation for a fruit salad! Any seasonal fruit will do. Experiment and use your imagination to arrange the fruit on the platter any way you like. Have fun!

Fresh Fruit Salad

APRICOT DRESSING

Dried apricots	8	8
Boiling water		
Vanilla yogurt	3/4 cup	175 mL
Fresh strawberries, halved	6	6
Kiwifruit, each cut lengthwise into 6 wedges	4	4
Seedless red grapes, halved	18	18
Cantaloupe balls or cubes	24	24
Fresh blueberries	1/2 cup	125 mL
Thin red apple wedges (with peel), dipped in lemon juice	12	12

Apricot Dressing: Put apricots into small bowl. Cover with boiling water. Let stand for about 20 minutes until softened. Drain. Transfer to blender or food processor. Add yogurt. Process until smooth. Makes about 3/4 cup (175 mL) dressing.

Arrange strawberries in centre of large serving platter. Arrange next 4 fruits in circular pattern around strawberries (see photo, page 77).

Place apple wedges, peel-side up, between fruit on platter. Drizzle dressing over salad or serve as dip on the side. Serves 6.

1 serving: 344 Calories; 1.7 g Total Fat (0.4 g Mono, 0.2 g Poly, 0.5 g Sat); 2 mg Cholesterol; 85 g Carbohydrate; 11 g Fibre; 6 g Protein; 40 mg Sodium

Pictured on page 77.

A healthy salad that's perfect for breakfast, brunch or lunch.

Summer Fruit Salad

Medium bananas, sliced	2	2
Honeydew balls	1 cup	250 mL
Fresh raspberries	1 cup	250 mL
Fresh blueberries	1 cup	250 mL
Fresh peach slices	1/2 cup	125 mL
Halved fresh strawberries	1/2 cup	125 mL

(continued on next page)

| 2% cottage cheese | 3 cups | 750 mL |
| Bread slices, toasted and halved diagonally (buttered, optional) | 6 | 6 |

SUMMER FRUIT TOPPING

| Frozen whipped topping, thawed | 1 cup | 250 mL |
| Light salad dressing (or light mayonnaise) | 4 tsp. | 20 mL |

Combine first 6 ingredients in large bowl.

Spoon cottage cheese onto centre of 6 salad plates. Spoon fruit mixture halfway around cottage cheese. Place 2 toast halves on opposite side of cottage cheese on each plate.

Summer Fruit Topping: Fold whipped topping into salad dressing in small bowl. Makes about 1 cup (250 mL) topping. Spoon over fruit. Serves 6.

1 serving: 307 Calories; 7.9 g Total Fat (1.8 g Mono, 0.7 g Poly, 4.7 g Sat); 10 mg Cholesterol; 41 g Carbohydrate; 4 g Fibre; 20 g Protein; 653 mg Sodium

Pictured below.

Full of colour and flavour, this pasta salad will dress up your meal or add pizzazz to your picnic.

about pesto

Classic Italian pesto is a rich, uncooked sauce made of crushed fresh basil, garlic, pine nuts, Parmesan cheese and olive oil. Pesto, including a sun-dried tomato variation, is available in most grocery stores.

Pesto Pasta Salad

Fusilli (or other spiral) pasta (about 1 lb., 454 g)	4 cups	1 L
Boiling water	16 cups	4 L
Salt	2 tsp.	10 mL
Cooked broccoli florets, chilled (see Note)	2 cups	500 mL
Cooked cauliflower florets, chilled	2 cups	500 mL
Cooked trimmed snow peas, chilled	2 cups	500 mL
Cooked sliced carrot, chilled	1 1/2 cups	375 mL
Sliced fresh white mushrooms	1 cup	250 mL
PESTO DRESSING		
Basil pesto	3/4 cup	175 mL
Olive (or cooking) oil	2/3 cup	150 mL
Grated Parmesan cheese	1/2 cup	125 mL
White vinegar	1/3 cup	75 mL
Salt	1 tsp.	5 mL

Cook pasta in boiling water and salt in large uncovered pot or Dutch oven for 8 to 10 minutes, stirring occasionally, until tender but firm. Drain. Rinse with cold water. Drain well. Transfer to large bowl.

Add next 5 ingredients. Toss.

Pesto Dressing: Combine all 5 ingredients in small bowl. Makes about 2 cups (500 mL) dressing. Drizzle over salad. Toss gently. Serves 8.

1 serving: 498 Calories; 26.2 g Total Fat (17.5 g Mono, 2.6 g Poly, 4.6 g Sat); 5 mg Cholesterol; 53 g Carbohydrate; 5 g Fibre; 14 g Protein; 462 mg Sodium

Pictured on page 81.

Note: Cook all vegetables just until tender-crisp for best results.

An inviting salad with a hearty helping of tasty ingredients. This Greek and Italian blend is sure to impress!

tip

To toast pine nuts, spread them in a single layer in an ungreased shallow pan. Bake in a 350°F (175°C) oven for 5 to 10 minutes, stirring or shaking often, until desired doneness.

Spinach Pasta Salad

Lemon juice	2 tbsp.	30 mL
Olive (or cooking) oil	1 tbsp.	15 mL
Garlic clove, minced (or 1/4 tsp., 1 mL, powder)	1	1
Boneless, skinless chicken breast halves	1/2 lb.	225 g
Medium bow (or other) pasta (about 6 oz., 170 g)	2 cups	500 mL
Boiling water	8 cups	2 L
Salt	1 tsp.	5 mL
Fresh spinach, stems removed, lightly packed	4 cups	1 L
Chopped tomato	1 cup	250 mL
Crumbled feta cheese (about 2 1/2 oz., 70 g)	1/2 cup	125 mL
Kalamata olives	1/3 cup	75 mL
PARSLEY PESTO DRESSING		
Coarsely chopped fresh parsley	1/2 cup	125 mL
Grated Parmesan cheese	1/3 cup	75 mL
Olive (or cooking) oil	1/3 cup	75 mL
Pine nuts, toasted (see Tip)	1/4 cup	60 mL
Red wine vinegar	1/4 cup	60 mL
Garlic cloves, minced (or 1/2 tsp., 2 mL, powder)	2	2
Salt	1/4 tsp.	1 mL
Pepper	1/8 tsp.	0.5 mL

Combine lemon juice, olive oil and garlic in medium bowl. Add chicken. Turn until coated. Preheat electric grill for 5 minutes or gas barbecue to medium (see Note). Cook chicken on greased grill for about 5 minutes per side until no longer pink inside. Transfer to large plate. Let stand for 10 minutes. Cut into 1/8 inch (3 mm) slices. Cover to keep warm.

Cook pasta in boiling water and salt in large uncovered pot or Dutch oven for 8 to 10 minutes, stirring occasionally, until tender but firm. Drain. Rinse with cold water. Drain well. Transfer to large bowl.

(continued on next page)

Add chicken and next 4 ingredients. Toss gently.

Parsley Pesto Dressing: Process all 8 ingredients in blender or food processor until smooth. Makes about 2/3 cup (150 mL) dressing. Drizzle over salad. Toss gently. Serves 6.

1 serving: 398 Calories; 24.6 g Total Fat (13.9 g Mono, 3.3 g Poly, 5.8 g Sat); 37 mg Cholesterol; 28 g Carbohydrate; 3 g Fibre; 20 g Protein; 413 mg Sodium

Pictured below.

Note: Chicken may be broiled in the oven instead of grilled. Place chicken on a greased broiler pan. Broil on the top rack for about 5 minutes per side until no longer pink inside.

A refreshing, satisfying dish. Lovely for lunch.

variation

Instead of ham flakes, use the same amount of canned tuna. Just as tasty!

Stuffed Tomato Salad

Large tomatoes	6	6
Orzo (or other very small pasta)	1 cup	250 mL
Boiling water	6 cups	1.5 L
Salt	3/4 tsp.	4 mL
Light salad dressing (or light mayonnaise)	1/4 cup	60 mL
Grated red onion	2 tbsp.	30 mL
Prepared mustard	2 tsp.	10 mL
Chopped fresh dill (or 1/4 tsp., 1 mL, dill weed)	1 tsp.	5 mL
Pepper, sprinkle		
Can of flaked ham, drained	6 1/2 oz.	184 g
Diced celery	1/2 cup	125 mL
Diced green pepper	1/4 cup	60 mL
Jar of pimiento, well drained and chopped	2 oz.	57 mL
Green onions, chopped	2	2

Slice 1/2 inch (12 mm) from top of each tomato. Using teaspoon, carefully scoop out pulp and seeds (see Note). Invert tomatoes on large plate to drain.

Cook orzo in boiling water and salt in large uncovered saucepan, stirring occasionally, until tender but firm. Drain. Rinse with cold water. Drain well.

Combine next 5 ingredients in medium bowl.

Add orzo and remaining 5 ingredients. Stir. Spoon into each tomato. Makes 6 stuffed tomatoes.

1 stuffed tomato: 265 Calories; 6.3 g Total Fat (2.8 g Mono, 1.6 g Poly, 1.1 g Sat); 14 mg Cholesterol; 41 g Carbohydrate; 3 g Fibre; 12 g Protein; 455 mg Sodium

Pictured on page 85.

Note: Use the pulp and seeds from the tomatoes in your favourite pasta sauce recipe.

Tried and true—the perfect side for a picnic or barbecue.

Main Macaroni Salad

Elbow macaroni	2 cups	500 mL
Boiling water	8 cups	2 L
Salt	1 tsp.	5 mL
Chopped celery	3/4 cup	175 mL
Sweet pickle relish	2 tbsp.	30 mL
Grated onion (or chopped green onion)	2 tbsp.	30 mL
Large hard-cooked eggs, chopped (optional)	2	2
Salad dressing (or mayonnaise)	3/4 cup	175 mL
Salt	1 tsp.	5 mL
Pepper	1/4 tsp.	1 mL

Radish slices, for garnish

Cook macaroni in boiling water and first amount of salt in large uncovered pot or Dutch oven for 8 to 10 minutes, stirring occasionally, until tender but firm. Drain. Rinse with cold water. Drain well. Transfer to large bowl.

Add next 4 ingredients. Stir.

Combine salad dressing, second amount of salt and pepper in small bowl. Add to macaroni mixture. Stir well. Chill until cold.

Garnish with radish slices. Serves 6.

1 serving: 302 Calories; 15.9 g Total Fat (8.5 g Mono, 5.3 g Poly, 1.2 g Sat); 8 mg Cholesterol; 34 g Carbohydrate; 1 g Fibre; 5 g Protein; 648 mg Sodium

Pictured on page 89.

Pine nuts and a dressing made with buttermilk make this salad deliciously different—the shrimp makes it company fare.

Shrimp Pasta Salad

Medium bow (or other) pasta (about 7 1/2 oz., 214 g)	2 1/2 cups	625 mL
Boiling water	8 cups	2 L
Salt	1 tsp.	5 mL

(continued on next page)

Bag of frozen cooked medium shrimp (peeled and deveined), thawed	12 oz.	340 g
Finely chopped red pepper	1/2 cup	125 mL
Pine nuts, toasted (see Tip)	1/2 cup	125 mL
Finely chopped celery	1/3 cup	75 mL
Finely chopped green onion	1/4 cup	60 mL

BUTTERMILK DRESSING

Buttermilk	1/2 cup	125 mL
Sour cream	1/4 cup	60 mL
Chopped fresh dill (or 1 1/4 tsp., 6 mL, dill weed)	1 1/2 tbsp.	25 mL
White wine vinegar	1 tbsp.	15 mL
Granulated sugar	2 tsp.	10 mL
Creamed horseradish	2 tsp.	10 mL
Salt	1/4 tsp.	1 mL
Pepper, just a pinch		

tip

To toast pine nuts, spread them in a single layer in an ungreased shallow pan. Bake in a 350°F (175°C) oven for 5 to 10 minutes, stirring or shaking often, until desired doneness.

Cook pasta in boiling water and salt in large uncovered pot or Dutch oven for 8 to 10 minutes, stirring occasionally, until tender but firm. Drain. Rinse with cold water. Drain well. Transfer to large bowl.

Add next 5 ingredients. Toss.

Buttermilk Dressing: Process all 8 ingredients in blender or food processor until smooth. Makes about 1 cup (250 mL) dressing. Drizzle over salad. Toss well. Serves 6.

1 serving: 298 Calories; 10 g Total Fat (3.3 g Mono, 3.6 g Poly, 2.4 g Sat); 115 mg Cholesterol; 33 g Carbohydrate; 4 g Fibre; 21 g Protein; 265 mg Sodium

Pictured below.

No need to toss out leftover pasta—toss it into a salad instead! A tasty blend of sweet and savoury flavours.

about dijon mustard

This strong-flavoured, pale yellow mustard gets its name from its city of origin, Dijon, France. A combination of mustard seeds, white wine and spices, Dijon mustard may be smooth, or grainy with whole seeds. French mustard labelled Dijon must adhere to strict standards. Contributing to its renowned quality are the brown mustard seeds imported from Canada. In fact, Canada provides approximately 95% of all of France's mustard needs.

Leftover Pasta Salad

Leftover cooked pasta (see Note)	1 cup	250 mL
Halved seedless green (or red) grapes	1/2 cup	125 mL
Diced medium Cheddar cheese	1/3 cup	75 mL
Diced deli ham	1/4 cup	60 mL
Sliced green onion	1 tbsp.	15 mL
CIDER DRESSING		
Mayonnaise (or salad dressing)	2 tbsp.	30 mL
Sour cream	2 tbsp.	30 mL
Dijon mustard (with whole seeds)	2 tsp.	10 mL
Apple cider vinegar	1 1/2 tsp.	7 mL
Granulated sugar	1/4 tsp.	1 mL
Salt	1/8 tsp.	0.5 mL
Pepper, sprinkle		
Dill weed, sprinkle		

Put first 5 ingredients into medium bowl. Toss.

Cider Dressing: Combine all 8 ingredients in small bowl. Chill for at least 10 minutes to blend flavours. Makes about 1/3 cup (75 mL) dressing. Drizzle over salad. Toss well. Serves 2.

1 serving: 367 Calories; 22.8 g Total Fat (9.7 g Mono, 4.7 g Poly, 7.3 g Sat); 45 mg Cholesterol; 28 g Carbohydrate; 1 g Fibre; 13 g Protein; 683 mg Sodium

Pictured on page 89.

Note: Coarsely chop long or very large pasta before measuring.

Top: Main Macaroni Salad, page 86
Bottom: Leftover Pasta Salad, above

A refreshing, Asian-style salad with a tasty peanut and lime dressing.

tip

To toast sesame seeds, spread them in a single layer in an ungreased shallow pan. Bake in a 350°F (175°C) oven for 5 to 10 minutes, stirring or shaking often, until desired doneness. Don't be afraid to toast more than you need. Just freeze the extra in an airtight container for the next time.

Peanut Rice Noodle Salad

Package of small rice stick noodles (9 oz., 250 g, size)	1/2	1/2
Boiling water		
Salt	1/2 tsp.	2 mL
English cucumber (with peel), thinly sliced	1	1
Red medium pepper, julienned (see Note)	1	1
Medium carrots, julienned	2	2
Snow peas, trimmed and julienned	1 1/2 cups	375 mL
Fresh bean sprouts	1 cup	250 mL
Thinly sliced red onion	1 cup	250 mL
Large hard-cooked eggs, quartered lengthwise	6	6
PEANUT DRESSING		
Smooth peanut butter	1/2 cup	125 mL
Peanut (or cooking) oil	1/4 cup	60 mL
Warm water	1/4 cup	60 mL
Lime juice	3 tbsp.	50 mL
Sweet (or regular) chili sauce	2 tbsp.	30 mL
Brown sugar, packed	2 tsp.	10 mL
Fish sauce	1 tsp.	5 mL
Finely grated, peeled gingerroot (or 1/8 tsp., 0.5 mL, ground ginger)	1/2 tsp.	2 mL
Garlic clove, minced (or 1/4 tsp., 1 mL, powder)	1	1
Salted peanuts	2/3 cup	150 mL
Chopped fresh mint leaves (or 1 1/2 tsp., 7 mL, dried)	2 tbsp.	30 mL
Sesame seeds, toasted (see Tip)	1 tbsp.	15 mL

Place noodles in large heatproof bowl. Cover with boiling water. Add salt. Stir until salt is dissolved. Let stand for about 20 minutes until softened. Drain well. Transfer to extra-large bowl.

(continued on next page)

Add next 6 ingredients. Toss. Remove to large serving platter.

Arrange egg on top of noodle mixture.

Peanut Dressing: Beat first 9 ingredients with whisk in medium bowl until smooth. Makes about 1 1/3 cups (325 mL) dressing. Drizzle over salad.

Scatter remaining 3 ingredients over top. Serves 8.

1 serving: 486 Calories; 27.4 g Total Fat (12.4 g Mono, 7.6 g Poly, 5.2 g Sat); 162 mg Cholesterol; 47 g Carbohydrate; 5 g Fibre; 17 g Protein; 347 mg Sodium

Pictured below.

Note: To julienne vegetables, cut into very thin strips that resemble matchsticks.

A lively combination of sweet and spicy ingredients. Crunchy cucumber and soft dates add an interesting texture to this zesty dish. Add extra mint to suit your taste, and serve on a bed of lettuce.

about couscous

Though it looks like rice, this staple of North African cuisine is actually tiny, pellet-like pasta made from Durum wheat semolina. While traditional cooking methods are rather complex, today's packaged versions, available in the rice section of your grocery store, are precooked and very easy to prepare. Some brands include their own seasonings or have been infused with different flavours such as tomato or garlic.

Plain couscous can be flavoured with broth, olive oil, herbs, peppers, olives, green onions—virtually anything you can think of, including fruit and nuts. Keep couscous on hand for use in salads, or to serve instead of potatoes, rice or noodles with just about anything!

Cucumber And Couscous Salad

Couscous	1 cup	250 mL
Boiling water	1 cup	250 mL
Olive (or cooking) oil	1 tbsp.	15 mL
Salt	1/4 tsp.	1 mL
Chopped English cucumber (with peel)	2 cups	500 mL
Coarsely grated zucchini (with peel)	1 cup	250 mL
Chopped pitted dates	2/3 cup	150 mL
Chopped green onion	1/2 cup	125 mL
Chopped fresh mint leaves (or 3/4 tsp., 4 mL, dried)	1 tbsp.	15 mL
CHILI DRESSING		
Olive (or cooking) oil	1/4 cup	60 mL
White wine vinegar	2 tbsp.	30 mL
Liquid honey	1 tbsp.	15 mL
Chili powder	1/2 tsp.	2 mL
Salt	1/4 tsp.	1 mL
Pepper	1/8 tsp.	0.5 mL

Combine first 4 ingredients in large heatproof bowl. Cover. Let stand for 5 minutes. Fluff with fork.

Add next 5 ingredients. Stir.

Chili Dressing: Combine all 6 ingredients in jar with tight-fitting lid. Shake well. Makes about 1/2 cup (125 mL) dressing. Drizzle over salad. Toss well. Serves 6.

1 serving: 308 Calories; 12.3 g Total Fat (8.8 g Mono, 1.1 g Poly, 1.7 g Sat); 0 mg Cholesterol; 46 g Carbohydrate; 4 g Fibre; 5 g Protein; 207 mg Sodium

Pictured on page 93.

Now this really is different. Go ahead and try it—you'll be glad you did!

Sweet Potato Salad

Olive (or cooking) oil	2 tbsp.	30 mL
Reserved pineapple juice	2 tbsp.	30 mL
Lemon juice	1 tbsp.	15 mL
Salt	1/2 tsp.	2 mL
Onion salt	1/4 tsp.	1 mL
Cubed cooked, peeled sweet potato	3 cups	750 mL
Can of pineapple tidbits, drained and juice reserved	14 oz.	398 mL
Chopped celery	3/4 cup	175 mL
Slivered almonds	1/4 cup	60 mL

Combine first 5 ingredients in large bowl.

Add sweet potato. Stir until coated. Cover. Chill for at least 1 hour to blend flavours.

Add pineapple, celery and almonds. Stir. Serves 10.

1 serving: 106 Calories; 4.8 g Total Fat (2.8 g Mono, 1.3 g Poly, 0.4 g Sat); 0 mg Cholesterol; 15 g Carbohydrate; 2 g Fibre; 2 g Protein; 164 mg Sodium

Pictured on page 99.

Tabbouleh (pronounced ta-BOO-lee) comes from the Middle East. Start with a little mint and add more to taste.

variation

Although our version allows for dried herbs, only fresh herbs—and lots of them—will do for a traditional tabbouleh! To make this tabbouleh truly classic, use the larger amount of fresh mint and increase the fresh parsley to 1 cup (250 mL).

Tabbouleh

Bulgur, fine grind	1 cup	250 mL
Boiling water	1 cup	250 mL
Medium tomatoes, diced	3	3
Green onions, chopped	3	3
Olive (or cooking) oil	1/4 cup	60 mL
Lemon juice	2 tbsp.	30 mL
Chopped fresh mint leaves (or 3/4 – 1 1/2 tsp., 4 – 7 mL, dried)	1 – 2 tbsp.	15 – 30 mL
Finely chopped fresh parsley (or 1/4 tsp., 1 mL, flakes)	1 1/2 tsp.	7 mL
Salt	1 tsp.	5 mL
Pepper	1/4 tsp.	1 mL
Ground allspice	1/8 tsp.	0.5 mL

(continued on next page)

Measure bulgur into large heatproof bowl. Add boiling water. Cover. Let stand for about 15 minutes until water is absorbed.

Add remaining 9 ingredients. Stir well. Serves 4.

1 serving: 277 Calories; 15.2 g Total Fat (10.7 g Mono, 1.5 g Poly, 2.1 g Sat); 0 mg Cholesterol; 33 g Carbohydrate; 5 g Fibre; 5 g Protein; 609 mg Sodium

Pictured below.

Fresh mint and cashews add an unexpected flair to this potato salad. The light, slightly sweet dressing will have them asking for more.

tip

To toast cashews, spread them in a single layer in an ungreased shallow pan. Bake in a 350°F (175°C) oven for 5 to 10 minutes, stirring or shaking often, until desired doneness.

Potato Mint Salad

Red medium potatoes (with skin), about 3 lbs. (1.4 kg)	6	6
Water		
Finely chopped red pepper	1/2 cup	125 mL
Raw cashews, toasted (see Tip), optional	3 tbsp.	50 mL
CREAMY MINT DRESSING		
Sour cream	1/2 cup	125 mL
Coarsely chopped fresh mint leaves	1/4 cup	60 mL
Liquid honey	2 tbsp.	30 mL
Lemon juice	2 tbsp.	30 mL
Dry mustard	2 tsp.	10 mL
Salt	1/2 tsp.	2 mL
Pepper	1/2 tsp.	2 mL
Chopped fresh chives (optional)	2 tbsp.	30 mL

Cook whole potatoes in water in large pot or Dutch oven until just tender. Drain. Let stand until cool enough to handle. Cut each potato in half lengthwise. Cut each half crosswise into 1/2 inch (12 mm) slices. Put into large bowl.

Add red pepper and cashews. Stir.

Creamy Mint Dressing: Process first 7 ingredients in blender or food processor until smooth. Makes about 3/4 cup (175 mL) dressing. Drizzle over salad. Stir well.

Sprinkle with chives. Serves 6.

1 serving: 174 Calories; 3.4 g Total Fat (1.1 g Mono, 0.3 g Poly, 1.8 g Sat); 8 mg Cholesterol; 33 g Carbohydrate; 3 g Fibre; 4 g Protein; 218 mg Sodium

Pictured on page 97.

A time-honoured classic and one of the best.

about potatoes

The many varieties of potatoes are categorized by their best use: baking, boiling and all-purpose. Baking potatoes, higher in starch than moisture, are dry and mealy when baked and are best used for mashed potato salads. Boiling potatoes, higher in moisture than starch, hold their shape when boiled—excellent for cutting up for potato salads. All-purpose potatoes are somewhere in-between.

Potato Salad

Cubed cooked, peeled potato	6 cups	1.5 L
Large hard-cooked eggs, chopped	4	4
Chopped celery	1 cup	250 mL
Sliced radish	1/4 cup	60 mL
Green onions, chopped	4	4
Chopped fresh parsley (or 1 tsp., 5 mL, flakes)	1 1/2 tbsp.	25 mL
Salad dressing (or mayonnaise)	1 cup	250 mL
Milk	1/4 cup	60 mL
Apple cider vinegar	1 tbsp.	15 mL
Granulated sugar	2 tsp.	10 mL
Prepared mustard	1 tsp.	5 mL
Salt	1 1/2 tsp.	7 mL
Pepper	1/4 tsp.	1 mL
Onion powder	1/4 tsp.	1 mL

Paprika, sprinkle
Sprig of fresh dill, for garnish

Put first 6 ingredients into large bowl. Stir.

Combine next 8 ingredients in small bowl. Drizzle over salad. Stir well. Cover. Chill for at least 2 hours to blend flavours.

Sprinkle with paprika. Garnish with dill. Serves 10.

1 serving: 250 Calories; 14.5 g Total Fat (7.6 g Mono, 4.4 g Poly, 1.6 g Sat); 93 mg Cholesterol; 25 g Carbohydrate; 2 g Fibre; 5 g Protein; 563 mg Sodium

Pictured on page 99.

This salad is a perfect way to use up leftover mashed potatoes, and a great reason to plan a picnic for two!

Mashed Potato Salad

Large hard-cooked egg, chopped	1	1
Salad dressing (or mayonnaise)	1/3 cup	75 mL
Diced celery	1/4 cup	60 mL
Green onion, sliced	1	1
Sweet pickle relish	2 tsp.	10 mL
Onion powder	1/8 tsp.	0.5 mL
Salt	1/8 tsp.	0.5 mL

(continued on next page)

Mashed potatoes	1 cup	250 mL
Large hard-cooked egg, sliced	1	1
Paprika, sprinkle		

Combine first 7 ingredients in medium bowl.

Add mashed potatoes. Stir. Remove to small serving bowl.

Arrange egg slices on top of salad. Sprinkle with paprika. Cover. Chill for 1 hour to blend flavours. Serves 2.

1 serving: 409 Calories; 25.7 g Total Fat (13.2 g Mono, 7.5 g Poly, 3.1 g Sat); 226 mg Cholesterol; 36 g Carbohydrate; 2 g Fibre; 9 g Protein; 535 mg Sodium

Pictured below.

Top: Potato Salad, page 98
Bottom right: Sweet Potato Salad, page 94
Bottom left: Mashed Potato Salad, page 98

You'll love the mild curry vinaigrette in this salad. It perfectly complements the shrimp and rice.

Best Rice Salad

Cold cooked rice (about 2/3 cup, 150 mL, uncooked), see Note	2 cups	500 mL
Chopped celery	1 1/2 cups	375 mL
Fresh (or frozen, thawed) peas	1 cup	250 mL
Can of small shrimp, drained	4 oz.	113 g
Finely chopped green onion	1/4 cup	60 mL
CURRY VINAIGRETTE		
Cooking (or olive) oil	1/2 cup	125 mL
White vinegar	3 tbsp.	50 mL
Soy sauce	2 tbsp.	30 mL
Curry powder	1 1/2 – 2 tsp.	7 – 10 mL
Granulated sugar	1/2 tsp.	2 mL
Celery salt	1/2 tsp.	2 mL

Combine first 5 ingredients in large bowl.

Curry Vinaigrette: Combine all 6 ingredients in jar with tight-fitting lid. Shake well. Makes about 7/8 cup (200 mL) dressing. Drizzle over salad. Stir gently. Serves 4 to 6.

1 serving: 465 Calories; 29.7 g Total Fat (17.1 g Mono, 8.8 g Poly, 2.2 g Sat); 23 mg Cholesterol; 41 g Carbohydrate; 1 g Fibre; 10 g Protein; 740 mg Sodium

Note: For added flavour, use brown or jasmine rice.

A quick and easy-to-make hot potato salad with an Italian flair.

Italian Hot Potato Salad

Bacon slices, diced	6	6
Cubed cooked potato	4 cups	1 L
Green onions, sliced	4	4
Chopped celery	1/2 cup	125 mL
Italian dressing	1/2 cup	125 mL
Grated Parmesan cheese	1/2 cup	125 mL

(continued on next page)

Cook bacon in large frying pan until crisp. Transfer with slotted spoon to paper towels to drain. Set aside. Discard drippings, reserving about 1 tsp. (5 mL) in pan.

Heat drippings on medium. Add next 4 ingredients. Heat and stir for about 8 minutes until heated through. Transfer to large bowl.

Add bacon and Parmesan cheese. Stir. Serve immediately. Serves 4.

1 serving: 438 Calories; 30.3 g Total Fat (15.3 g Mono, 7.9 g Poly, 5.7 g Sat); 39 mg Cholesterol; 32 g Carbohydrate; 3 g Fibre; 12 g Protein; 911 mg Sodium

Pictured below.

A great way to use up leftover rice and veggies. Stuff this salad into a pita pocket for a tasty sandwich.

variation

For extra goodness, add 2 tbsp. (30 mL) sunflower seeds or shelled pumpkin seeds, or add up to 1/4 cup (60 mL) raisins.

Rice Salad

Cold cooked rice (about 1/4 cup, 60 mL, uncooked)	3/4 cup	175 mL
Cold cooked vegetables (such as peas, broccoli florets or green beans)	1/2 cup	125 mL
Chopped cooked ham	1/3 cup	75 mL
Grated carrot	1/4 cup	60 mL
Sliced green onion	2 tbsp.	30 mL
White vinegar (see Note)	2 tsp.	10 mL
Olive (or cooking) oil	1 tsp.	5 mL
Salt, sprinkle		

Combine all 8 ingredients in small bowl. Serves 2.

1 serving: 198 Calories; 4.9 g Total Fat (2.9 g Mono, 0.7 g Poly, 1.2 g Sat); 14 mg Cholesterol; 29 g Carbohydrate; 2 g Fibre; 9 g Protein; 380 mg Sodium

Pictured on page 103.

Note: If preferred, use the same amount of white wine vinegar or apple cider vinegar instead of white vinegar.

Bright, crispy vegetables together with rice and pineapple in one delicious salad. Coconut adds the final tropical touch!

Crunchy Rice Salad

Cold cooked long grain white rice (about 2/3 cup, 150 mL, uncooked), see Note	2 cups	500 mL
Can of pineapple tidbits, drained	14 oz.	398 mL
Can of sliced water chestnuts, drained and chopped	8 oz.	227 mL
Diced celery	1/2 cup	125 mL
Diced red pepper	1/2 cup	125 mL
Diced red onion	1/2 cup	125 mL
LIME DRESSING		
Lime juice	3 tbsp.	50 mL
Cooking (or olive) oil	1 tbsp.	15 mL
Low-sodium soy sauce	1 tbsp.	15 mL
Sweet chili sauce	1 tbsp.	15 mL

(continued on next page)

Shredded (long thread) or flake coconut, 1/4 cup 60 mL
   toasted (see Tip), optional

Combine first 6 ingredients in large bowl.

Lime Dressing: Combine first 4 ingredients in jar with tight-fitting lid. Shake well. Makes about 1/3 cup (75 mL) dressing. Drizzle over salad. Stir.

Sprinkle with coconut. Serves 6.

1 serving: 172 Calories; 2.7 g Total Fat (1.4 g Mono, 0.8 g Poly, 0.2 g Sat); 0 mg Cholesterol; 34 g Carbohydrate; 2 g Fibre; 3 g Protein; 134 mg Sodium

Pictured below.

Note: For an authentic Asian flavour, use jasmine or basmati rice.

tip

To toast coconut, spread in a single layer in an ungreased shallow pan. Bake in a 350°F (175°C) oven for 5 to 10 minutes, stirring or shaking often, until desired doneness.

Top: Crunchy Rice Salad, page 102
Bottom left and bottom right: Rice Salad, page 102

A basic oil and vinegar dressing that's delicious on any combination of salad greens and vegetables.

Vinaigrette

Olive (or cooking) oil	6 tbsp.	100 mL
Apple cider (or red wine) vinegar	3 tbsp.	50 mL
Granulated sugar	1 tsp.	5 mL
Paprika	1/2 tsp.	2 mL
Onion salt	1/4 tsp.	1 mL
Pepper, sprinkle		

Combine all 6 ingredients in jar with tight-fitting lid. Shake well. Store in refrigerator for up to 2 weeks. Shake well before drizzling over salad. Makes about 1/2 cup (125 mL).

2 tbsp. (30 mL): 180 Calories; 19.7 g Total Fat (14.5 g Mono, 1.7 g Poly, 2.7 g Sat); 0 mg Cholesterol; 2 g Carbohydrate; 0 g Fibre; 0 g Protein; 74 mg Sodium

Pictured on page 105.

Great for tossing with mixed greens or for marinating vegetables.

tip

To reduce the fat content of any salad, simply use less dressing. Add just enough to flavour greens.

Italian Dressing

Olive (or cooking) oil	1 cup	250 mL
Lemon juice	1/4 cup	60 mL
White vinegar	1/4 cup	60 mL
Granulated sugar	2 tsp.	10 mL
Salt	1 tsp.	5 mL
Garlic salt	1/2 tsp.	2 mL
Onion salt	1/2 tsp.	2 mL
Dry mustard	1/2 tsp.	2 mL
Paprika	1/2 tsp.	2 mL
Dried oregano	1/2 tsp.	2 mL
Ground thyme	1/8 tsp.	0.5 mL

Combine all 11 ingredients in jar with tight-fitting lid. Shake well. Chill for 2 hours to blend flavours. Store in refrigerator for up to 2 weeks. Shake well before drizzling over salad. Makes about 1 1/2 cups (375 mL).

2 tbsp. (30 mL): 169 Calories; 18.5 g Total Fat (10.9 g Mono, 5.5 g Poly, 1.3 g Sat); 0 mg Cholesterol; 2 g Carbohydrate; 0 g Fibre; 0 g Protein; 285 mg Sodium

Pictured on page 105.

Photo legend
1. Italian Dressing, above
2. French Dressing, page 106
3. Cooked Salad Dressing, page 106
4. Vinaigrette, this page
5. Blue Cheese Dressing, page 107

A favourite from way, way back. With the consistency of mayonnaise, this thick, tangy dressing is best for potato salads, coleslaws, chunky vegetable or pasta salads, or salads made with iceberg lettuce.

Cooked Salad Dressing

Granulated sugar	1/2 cup	125 mL
All-purpose flour	2 tbsp.	30 mL
Dry mustard	1 tbsp.	15 mL
Salt	1 tsp.	5 mL
Large eggs	3	3
Milk	1 cup	250 mL
White vinegar	1/2 cup	125 mL
Water	1/2 cup	125 mL

Combine first 4 ingredients in heavy medium saucepan. Add eggs 1 at a time, beating well after each addition.

Add milk, vinegar and water. Heat and stir on medium for 10 to 12 minutes until boiling and thickened. Cool slightly. Transfer to airtight container. Store in refrigerator for up to 3 weeks. Stir well before adding to salad. Makes about 2 1/2 cups (625 mL).

2 tbsp. (30 mL): 42 Calories; 1 g Total Fat (0.4 g Mono, 0.1 g Poly, 0.3 g Sat); 32 mg Cholesterol; 7 g Carbohydrate; 0 g Fibre; 2 g Protein; 129 mg Sodium

Pictured on page 105.

A tasty red dressing for your favourite tossed salad.

French Dressing

Can of condensed tomato soup	10 oz.	284 mL
Chopped onion	1/3 cup	75 mL
Apple cider vinegar	1/4 cup	60 mL
Granulated sugar	1/4 cup	60 mL
Olive (or cooking) oil	3 tbsp.	50 mL
Worcestershire sauce	3/4 tsp.	4 mL
Garlic clove, minced (or 1/4 tsp., 1 mL, powder)	1	1
Salt	1/4 tsp.	1 mL

Process all 8 ingredients in blender or food processor until smooth. Pour into jar with tight-fitting lid. Store in refrigerator for up to 1 week. Shake well before drizzling over salad. Makes about 2 cups (500 mL).

2 tbsp. (30 mL): 49 Calories; 2.8 g Total Fat (1.5 g Mono, 0.9 g Poly, 0.2 g Sat); 0 mg Cholesterol; 6 g Carbohydrate; 0 g Fibre; 0 g Protein; 164 mg Sodium

Pictured on page 105.

Blue Cheese Dressing

Light mayonnaise (or light salad dressing)	1 cup	250 mL
Crumbled blue cheese (about 4 oz.,113 g)	3/4 cup	175 mL
Light sour cream	1/2 cup	125 mL
White vinegar	1 tbsp.	15 mL
Seasoned salt	1 tsp.	5 mL
Salt	1/2 tsp.	2 mL
Pepper	1/4 tsp.	1 mL
Onion powder	1/4 tsp.	1 mL
Garlic clove, minced (or 1/4 tsp., 1 mL, powder)	1	1
Milk (optional)	2 tbsp.	30 mL

Process first 9 ingredients in blender or food processor until smooth.

Add milk. Process until just combined. Pour into jar with tight-fitting lid. Store in refrigerator for up to 1 week. Shake well before drizzling over salad. Makes about 2 cups (500 mL).

2 tbsp. (30 mL): 77 Calories; 7.1 g Total Fat (3.5 g Mono, 1.5 g Poly, 2.2 g Sat); 7 mg Cholesterol; 2 g Carbohydrate; 0 g Fibre; 2 g Protein; 340 mg Sodium

Pictured on page 105.

Blue cheese lovers will enjoy the tangy, pungent flavour of this one. Add or omit the milk depending on how thick you like your dressing. Delicious on mixed greens, or try it in potato salad.

Dijon Dressing

Olive (or cooking) oil	1/4 cup	60 mL
Dijon mustard	2 tbsp.	30 mL
Mayonnaise (or salad dressing)	1 tbsp.	15 mL
Red wine vinegar	1 tbsp.	15 mL
Lemon juice	1 tbsp.	15 mL
Brown sugar, packed	1 tsp.	5 mL
Salt	1/4 tsp.	1 mL

Combine all 7 ingredients in jar with tight-fitting lid. Shake well. Store in refrigerator for up to 1 week. Shake well before drizzling over salad. Makes about 1/2 cup (125 mL).

2 tbsp. (30 mL): 159 Calories; 17 g Total Fat (11.7 g Mono, 2.4 g Poly, 2.2 g Sat); 2 mg Cholesterol; 2 g Carbohydrate; 0 g Fibre; 1 g Protein; 260 mg Sodium

Pictured on page 109.

Dijon mustard is a classic flavouring in salad dressings and vinaigrettes. This one will add a zesty flavour to your mixed green salads. Also good used in a marinated veggie salad.

As an alternative to Caesar flavours, dress your romaine lettuce salad in this creamy dressing. A nice dressing for pasta salads, too!

Creamy Garlic Dressing

Light salad dressing (or light mayonnaise)	1/2 cup	125 mL
Milk	1/4 cup	60 mL
White vinegar	2 tsp.	10 mL
Garlic cloves, minced (or 1 tsp., 5 mL, powder)	4	4
Granulated sugar	1/2 tsp.	2 mL
Dry mustard	1/4 tsp.	1 mL
Onion powder	1/8 tsp.	0.5 mL
Salt	1/8 tsp.	0.5 mL
Pepper, sprinkle		

Combine all 9 ingredients in small bowl. Transfer to airtight container. Store in refrigerator for up to 1 week. Stir well before drizzling over salad. Makes about 3/4 cup (175 mL).

2 tbsp. (30 mL): 67 Calories; 5.2 g Total Fat (3 g Mono, 1.5 g Poly, 0.3 g Sat); 0 mg Cholesterol; 5 g Carbohydrate; 0 g Fibre; 1 g Protein; 208 mg Sodium

Pictured on page 109.

Also known as "Italian Vinaigrette," this dressing is delicious tossed with a mixture of salad greens and tomatoes.

storing olive oil

Olive oil is best stored in a cool, dark place, where it will keep for up to 6 months. It may be stored in the refrigerator for up to a year, but will become cloudy and too thick to pour. Room temperature will return it to a clear liquid, but we suggest you buy only as much as you will use in a short time.

Martini Dressing

Olive (or cooking) oil	2/3 cup	150 mL
White wine vinegar	6 tbsp.	100 mL
Grated Romano cheese	6 tbsp.	100 mL
Chopped fresh basil	1/4 cup	60 mL
Garlic cloves	6	6

Process all 5 ingredients in blender or food processor for about 1 minute until well combined. Pour into jar with tight-fitting lid. Store in refrigerator for up to 1 week. Shake well before drizzling over salad. Makes about 1 cup (250 mL).

2 tbsp. (30 mL): 185 Calories; 19.6 g Total Fat (13.9 g Mono, 1.6 g Poly, 3.3 g Sat); 5 mg Cholesterol; 2 g Carbohydrate; 0 g Fibre; 2 g Protein; 55 mg Sodium

Pictured on page 109.

Clockwise from centre left:
Dijon Dressing, page 107
Martini Dressing, above
Creamy Garlic Dressing, this page

Thick and pleasantly pink. A delectable complement to a spinach and fruit salad.

about vinaigrette

The standard ratio for basic vinaigrette—three parts oil to one part vinegar—is a good starting point when creating your own, however the ratio may be changed to suit personal taste. Experiment, using olive or cooking oil and vinegars such as red or white wine, apple cider or balsamic. Season with fresh herbs and spices, and let nothing but your imagination stop you!

Apple cider vinegar provides a fruity taste to this delicious vinaigrette. Great drizzled over a mixture of greens and cut-up fresh fruit.

Poppy Seed Dressing

Granulated sugar	3/4 cup	175 mL
White vinegar	1/3 cup	75 mL
Dry mustard	1 tsp.	5 mL
Onion flakes	1 tsp.	5 mL
Salt	1 tsp.	5 mL
Olive (or cooking) oil	1 cup	250 mL
Poppy seeds	1 1/2 tbsp.	25 mL
Drop of red liquid food colouring	1	1

Process first 5 ingredients in blender or food processor until smooth.

With motor running, add olive oil in thin stream through hole in lid until thickened. Pour into jar with tight-fitting lid.

Add poppy seeds and food colouring. Shake well. Store in refrigerator for up to 3 weeks. Shake well before drizzling over salad. Makes about 1 2/3 cups (400 mL).

2 tbsp. (30 mL): 197 Calories; 17 g Total Fat (9.8 g Mono, 5.2 g Poly, 1.2 g Sat); 0 mg Cholesterol; 12 g Carbohydrate; 0 g Fibre; 0 g Protein; 170 mg Sodium

Pictured on page 111.

Apple Cider Vinaigrette

Olive (or cooking) oil	6 tbsp.	100 mL
Apple cider vinegar	2 tbsp.	30 mL
Granulated sugar	1 tsp.	5 mL
Dry mustard	1 tsp.	5 mL
Garlic clove, minced (or 1/4 tsp., 1 mL, powder)	1	1
Salt	1 tsp.	5 mL
Pepper	1/2 tsp.	2 mL

Combine all 7 ingredients in jar with tight-fitting lid. Shake well. Store in refrigerator for up to 1 week. Shake well before drizzling over salad. Makes about 1/2 cup (125 mL).

2 tbsp. (30 mL): 186 Calories; 20.1 g Total Fat (11.9 g Mono, 5.9 g Poly, 1.4 g Sat); 0 mg Cholesterol; 2 g Carbohydrate; 0 g Fibre; 0 g Protein; 569 mg Sodium

Pictured on page 111.

Pink Dressing

Salad dressing (or mayonnaise)	1 cup	250 mL
Pineapple tidbits, drained	1 cup	250 mL
Granulated sugar	1/4 cup	60 mL
Chopped walnuts	1/4 cup	60 mL
Maraschino cherry syrup	1/4 cup	60 mL
Chopped maraschino cherries	1/4 cup	60 mL
Whipping cream	1/4 cup	60 mL

A delicious dressing to mix with fresh fruit or to spoon over spinach or lettuce leaves. Use it as a fruit dip, too!

Process first 6 ingredients in blender or food processor until smooth. Transfer to medium bowl.

Beat whipping cream in small bowl until stiff peaks form. Fold into pineapple mixture. Transfer to airtight container. Store in refrigerator for up to 1 week. Stir well before drizzling over salad. Makes about 2 cups (500 mL).

2 tbsp. (30 mL): 124 Calories; 9.7 g Total Fat (4.7 g Mono, 3.2 g Poly, 1.4 g Sat); 8 mg Cholesterol; 9 g Carbohydrate; trace Fibre; 1 g Protein; 95 mg Sodium

Pictured below.

Clockwise from top left:
Apple Cider Vinaigrette, page 110
Pink Dressing, above
Poppy Seed Dressing, page 110

Invigorate your favourite Asian-style salads with this tangy dressing.

about sesame oil

Sesame oil has a deep amber colour and a rich, nutty flavour. Because of its intense flavour, sesame oil is generally used in small amounts.

Ginger Dressing

Slice of gingerroot (1/2 inch, 12 mm, thick), peeled	1	1
Green onion, cut into 4 pieces	1	1
Baby carrot, halved	1	1
Garlic clove, minced (or 1/4 tsp., 1 mL, powder)	1	1
Cooking oil	1/2 cup	125 mL
Rice vinegar	1/3 cup	75 mL
Soy sauce	1 tbsp.	15 mL
Dry mustard	1/2 tsp.	2 mL
Sesame oil, for flavour (optional)	2 tsp.	10 mL

Process all 9 ingredients in blender or food processor for about 1 minute, scraping down sides if necessary, until smooth. Pour into jar with tight-fitting lid. Chill for 1 hour to blend flavours. Store in refrigerator for up to 1 week. Shake well before drizzling over salad. Makes about 1 cup (250 mL).

2 tbsp. (30 mL): 128 Calories; 13.9 g Total Fat (8.2 g Mono, 4.1 g Poly, 1 g Sat); 0 mg Cholesterol; 1 g Carbohydrate; 0 g Fibre; 0 g Protein; 126 mg Sodium

Pictured on page 113.

A sweet, fragrant dressing with a ginger and chili bite. Perfect tossed with dark leafy greens, or used as a dipping sauce for meatballs or chicken.

tip

To toast sesame seeds, spread them in a single layer in an ungreased shallow pan. Bake in a 350°F (175°C) oven for 5 to 10 minutes, stirring or shaking often, until desired doneness.

Sesame Soy Dressing

White vinegar	1/3 cup	75 mL
Indonesian sweet (or thick) soy sauce	1/4 cup	60 mL
Finely grated, peeled gingerroot (or 3/4 tsp., 4 mL, ground ginger)	1 tbsp.	15 mL
Brown sugar, packed	1 tbsp.	15 mL
Sesame seeds, toasted (see Tip)	1 tbsp.	15 mL
Sesame oil, for flavour	2 tsp.	10 mL
Dried crushed chilies	1/2 tsp.	2 mL
Cooking oil	1/4 cup	60 mL

(continued on next page)

Process first 7 ingredients in blender or food processor for about 5 seconds until foamy.

With motor running, add cooking oil in thin stream through hole in lid until well combined. Pour into jar with tight-fitting lid. Store in refrigerator for up to 1 week. Shake well before drizzling over salad. Makes about 1 cup (250 mL).

2 tbsp. (30 mL): 91 Calories; 8.7 g Total Fat (4.8 g Mono, 2.8 g Poly, 0.7 g Sat); 0 mg Cholesterol; 3 g Carbohydrate; trace Fibre; 1 g Protein; 417 mg Sodium

Pictured below.

Top: Ginger Dressing, page 112
Bottom: Sesame Soy Dressing, page 112

Only two ingredients, and low-fat, too! Toss it with orange segments in your favourite green salad, or add it to a fruit salad for a zesty finish.

Tangy Orange Dressing

Light salad dressing (or light mayonnaise)	2/3 cup	150 mL
Frozen concentrated orange juice, thawed	1/3 cup	75 mL

Combine salad dressing and concentrated orange juice in small bowl. Transfer to airtight container. Store in refrigerator for up to 1 week. Stir well before drizzling over salad. Makes about 1 cup (250 mL).

2 tbsp. (30 mL): 76 Calories; 5.1 g Total Fat (2.9 g Mono, 1.5 g Poly, 0.3 g Sat); 0 mg Cholesterol; 8 g Carbohydrate; trace Fibre; 0 g Protein; 154 mg Sodium

Pictured on page 115.

Fresh and light—perfect on delicate baby greens. Tangy and fruity, with no added fat!

Raspberry Dressing

Fresh (or frozen, thawed) raspberries	3 cups	750 mL
White vinegar	1 cup	250 mL
Granulated sugar	1 1/2 cups	375 mL

Combine raspberries and vinegar in small bowl. Cover. Chill for 48 hours.

Transfer raspberry mixture to medium saucepan. Add sugar. Stir. Bring to a boil on medium, stirring often. Reduce heat to medium-low. Simmer, uncovered, for 15 minutes without stirring. Cool slightly. Press raspberry mixture through sieve into medium bowl. Discard seeds. Pour into jar with tight-fitting lid. Store in refrigerator for up to 1 month. Shake well before drizzling over salad. Makes about 2 cups (500 mL).

2 tbsp. (30 mL): 87 Calories; 0.1 g Total Fat (0 g Mono, 0.1 g Poly, 0 g Sat); 0 mg Cholesterol; 22 g Carbohydrate; 1 g Fibre; 0 g Protein; 0 mg Sodium

Pictured on page 115.

Clockwise from top left:
Honey Mustard Dressing, page 116
Raspberry Dressing, above
Tangy Orange Dressing, this page
Cucumber Dressing, page 116
Thousand Island Dressing, page 117

A perfect blend of tangy and sweet flavours. This low-fat dressing adds lots of flavour to mixed greens.

Honey Mustard Dressing

Liquid honey	1/4 cup	60 mL
White vinegar	1/4 cup	60 mL
Prepared mustard	2 tsp.	10 mL
Cornstarch	2 tsp.	10 mL

Combine all 4 ingredients in small saucepan. Heat and stir on medium for about 8 minutes until boiling and thickened. Cool. Pour into jar with tight-fitting lid. Store in refrigerator for up to 1 week. Shake well before drizzling over salad. Makes about 1/2 cup (125 mL).

2 tbsp. (30 mL): 87 Calories; 0.2 g Total Fat (0 g Mono, 0.1 g Poly, 0 g Sat); 0 mg Cholesterol; 23 g Carbohydrate; 0 g Fibre; 0 g Protein; 39 mg Sodium

Pictured on page 115.

Cool cucumber and dill dressing is a great choice any time. Makes a nice dip for vegetable sticks, too!

Cucumber Dressing

Diced peeled English cucumber	1/2 cup	125 mL
Sour cream	1/3 cup	75 mL
Lemon juice	1 tsp.	5 mL
Chopped fresh parsley (or 1/4 tsp., 1 mL, flakes)	1 tsp.	5 mL
Chopped fresh dill (or 1/4 tsp., 1 mL, dill weed)	1 tsp.	5 mL
Salt	1/4 tsp.	1 mL

Combine all 6 ingredients in small bowl. Transfer to airtight container. Store in refrigerator for up to 1 week. Stir well before drizzling over salad. Makes about 3/4 cup (175 mL).

2 tbsp. (30 mL): 21 Calories; 1.8 g Total Fat (0.5 g Mono, 0.1 g Poly, 1.1 g Sat); 5 mg Cholesterol; 1 g Carbohydrate; 0 g Fibre; 0 g Protein; 100 mg Sodium

Pictured on page 115.

Thousand Island Dressing

Salad dressing (or mayonnaise)	3/4 cup	175 mL
Chili sauce	1/3 cup	75 mL
Sweet pickle relish	2 1/2 tbsp.	37 mL
Finely chopped onion	2 tsp.	10 mL
Large hard-cooked egg, chopped	1	1
Chopped pimiento	2 tsp.	10 mL

Combine first 4 ingredients in medium bowl.

Add egg and pimiento. Stir. Transfer to airtight container. Store in refrigerator for up to 2 days. Stir well before drizzling over salad. Makes about 1 1/3 cups (325 mL).

2 tbsp. (30 mL): 104 Calories; 8.8 g Total Fat (4.7 g Mono, 2.8 g Poly, 0.8 g Sat); 24 mg Cholesterol; 7 g Carbohydrate; trace Fibre; 1 g Protein; 254 mg Sodium

Pictured on page 115.

Always a favourite. Put a ladle in a bowl of this dressing and let guests help themselves.

Roasted Pecans

Hard margarine (or butter)	1 tbsp.	15 mL
Pecan halves	2 cups	500 mL
Worcestershire sauce	2 tbsp.	30 mL
Ketchup	2 tsp.	10 mL
Cayenne pepper	1/4 tsp.	1 mL

Salt, sprinkle

Melt margarine in large saucepan. Add next 4 ingredients. Stir until pecans are coated. Spread evenly in greased baking sheet with sides. Bake in 350°F (175°C) oven for 20 minutes, stirring every 5 minutes. Transfer to separate paper towel-lined baking sheet.

Sprinkle with salt. Cool. Store in airtight container at room temperature for up to 2 weeks. Makes about 2 cups (500 mL).

1/4 cup (60 mL): 206 Calories; 20.8 g Total Fat (13 g Mono, 4.9 g Poly, 1.9 g Sat); 0 mg Cholesterol; 6 g Carbohydrate; 2 g Fibre; 3 g Protein; 71 mg Sodium

When money is no object, these pecans turn a salad into a celebration.

This sweet and spicy nut mix is sure to please. Sprinkle it over fruit and spinach salads for a sweet, crunchy finish.

Spiced Nuts

Brown sugar, packed	1/2 cup	125 mL
Granulated sugar	1/2 cup	125 mL
Ground cinnamon	1 1/2 tsp.	7 mL
Ground nutmeg	1/2 tsp.	2 mL
Ground ginger	1/2 tsp.	2 mL
Ground cloves	1/4 tsp.	1 mL
Egg white (large)	1	1
Water	1 tbsp.	15 mL
Mixed nuts	4 cups	1 L

Combine first 6 ingredients in small bowl.

Beat egg white and water in medium bowl until frothy. Add brown sugar mixture. Stir well.

Add nuts. Stir until coated. Spread evenly in greased baking sheet with sides. Bake in 325°F (160°C) oven for about 20 minutes, stirring occasionally, until golden. Cool. Store in airtight container at room temperature for up to 2 weeks. Makes about 6 cups (1.5 L).

1/4 cup (60 mL): 180 Calories; 12.4 g Total Fat (7.6 g Mono, 2.6 g Poly, 1.7 g Sat); 0 mg Cholesterol; 15 g Carbohydrate; 1 g Fibre; 4 g Protein; 7 mg Sodium

Pictured on page 119.

Sprinkle this savoury mixture on a green leaf or noodle salad. Goes great with Ginger Dressing, page 112.

Sesame Walnut Topping

Finely chopped walnuts	2 tbsp.	30 mL
Sesame seeds	1 tbsp.	15 mL
Cumin seed	1/2 tsp.	2 mL

Heat and stir all 3 ingredients in small frying pan on medium for about 3 minutes until fragrant. Transfer to small custard cup. Cool. Store in airtight container at room temperature for up to 2 weeks. Makes about 3 tbsp. (50 mL).

1 tsp. (5 mL): 13 Calories; 1.2 g Total Fat (0.3 g Mono, 0.7 g Poly, 0.1 g Sat); 0 mg Cholesterol; 0 g Carbohydrate; trace Fibre; 0 g Protein; 0 mg Sodium

Pictured on page 119.

Clockwise from top left:
Spiced Nuts, this page
Basil Pesto Croutons, page 120
Sesame Walnut Topping, above

Beat the crouton blahs with these savoury morsels! Scatter them over your favourite tossed salad for a flavourful finishing crunch.

tomato pesto croutons

Instead of basil pesto, use the same amount of sun-dried tomato pesto.

Basil Pesto Croutons

Basil pesto	2 tbsp.	30 mL
Peanut (or cooking) oil	1 tbsp.	15 mL
Small dry bread cubes	1 cup	250 mL

Combine pesto and peanut oil in medium bowl. Add bread cubes. Toss until coated. Spread evenly in greased baking sheet with sides. Bake in 375°F (190°C) oven for about 10 minutes, stirring once, until golden and crisp. Cool. Store in airtight container at room temperature for up to 1 week. Makes about 1 cup (250 mL).

1/4 cup (60 mL): 75 Calories; 6.1 g Total Fat (3.4 g Mono, 1.4 g Poly, 1 g Sat); 0 mg Cholesterol; 5 g Carbohydrate; trace Fibre; 1 g Protein; 50 mg Sodium

Pictured on page 119.

These crispy, flavourful crackers are a cinch to make. A great way to encourage kids to eat their salad!

Little Dilled Snacks

Hard margarine (or butter)	1/2 cup	125 mL
Envelope of ranch dressing mix (1 oz., 28 g), stir before measuring	1/2	1/2
Chopped fresh dill (or 1 1/2 tsp., 7 mL, dill weed)	2 tbsp.	30 mL
Paprika	1/4 tsp.	1 mL
Plain-flavoured fish-shaped crackers	4 cups	1 L

Melt margarine in medium saucepan. Add dressing mix, dill and paprika. Stir well.

Put crackers into large bowl. Drizzle with dill mixture. Toss until coated. Spread evenly in ungreased baking sheet with sides. Bake in 300°F (150°C) oven for about 15 minutes, stirring after 10 minutes, until crisp and golden. Cool. Store in airtight container at room temperature for up to 2 weeks. Makes about 4 cups (1 L).

1/4 cup (60 mL): 124 Calories; 9.4 g Total Fat (5.4 g Mono, 1.7 g Poly, 1.9 g Sat); 0 mg Cholesterol; 9 g Carbohydrate; trace Fibre; 1 g Protein; 308 mg Sodium

Pictured on page 121.

Minted Pita Chips

Finely chopped fresh mint leaves (or 1 1/2 tsp., 7 mL, dried)	2 tbsp.	30 mL
Olive (or cooking) oil	2 tbsp.	30 mL
Sesame seeds, toasted (see Tip)	2 tsp.	10 mL
Poppy seeds	2 tsp.	10 mL
Salt	1/8 tsp.	0.5 mL
Pita breads (7 inch, 18 cm, diameter), split	3	3

Combine first 5 ingredients in small bowl.

Place pita bread rounds, inside-up, on greased baking sheet. Brush with mint mixture. Bake in 350°F (175°C) oven for about 10 minutes until crisp and golden. Cool. Break into irregular-shaped pieces, 2 to 3 inches (5 to 7.5 cm) each. Store in airtight container at room temperature for up to 2 weeks. Makes about 50 pita chips.

1 pita chip: 16 Calories; 0.7 g Total Fat (0.4 g Mono, 0.1 g Poly, 0.1 g Sat); 0 mg Cholesterol; 2 g Carbohydrate; 0 g Fibre; 0 g Protein; 26 mg Sodium

Pictured below.

Enliven your salads with fresh minty flavour and a poppy seed crunch. A tasty alternative to croutons.

tip

To toast sesame seeds, spread them in a single layer in an ungreased shallow pan. Bake in a 350°F (175°C) oven for 5 to 10 minutes, stirring or shaking often, until desired doneness. Don't be afraid to toast more than you need. Just freeze the extra in an airtight container for the next time.

Left: Minted Pita Chips, above
Right: Little Dilled Snacks, page 120

Pictured on page 123.

Marinated Onion Rings

Great in your favourite salad or grilled cheese sandwich. Jean serves this as a salad on its own.

tip

To keep your hands odour-free, rub them with a few drops of white vinegar before handling onions.

Large red or white onion, sliced paper-thin (see Note) and separated into rings	1	1
Cold water		
Water	3/4 cup	175 mL
Granulated sugar	3/4 cup	175 mL
White vinegar	3/4 cup	175 mL
Olive (or cooking) oil	1 tbsp.	15 mL
Salt	1/2 tsp.	2 mL
Pepper	1/8 tsp.	0.5 mL

Put onion rings into large heatproof bowl. Cover with cold water. Let stand for 1 hour. Drain.

Combine remaining 6 ingredients in small saucepan. Heat and stir on medium until boiling. Add to onion. Press onion with spoon into vinegar mixture. Cover. Chill for 24 hours to blend flavours. Store in refrigerator for up to 2 weeks. Serves 10.

1 serving: 82 Calories; 1.4 g Total Fat (0.8 g Mono, 0.4 g Poly, 0.1 g Sat); 0 mg Cholesterol; 18 g Carbohydrate; trace Fibre; 0 g Protein; 119 mg Sodium

Pictured on page 123.

Note: If you have one, an electric food slicer works best to achieve the thinnest possible onion slices.

Marinated Feta

Feta with red pepper, infused with savoury herbs and spices, makes a great salad topper.

Sprigs of fresh rosemary	3	3
Dried oregano	1 tbsp.	15 mL
Cumin seed	1 tbsp.	15 mL
Pepper	2 tsp.	10 mL
Red medium peppers, quartered	2	2
Cubed feta cheese	2 1/3 cups	575 mL
Olive (or cooking) oil	1/2 cup	125 mL

(continued on next page)

Combine first 4 ingredients in large bowl.

Arrange red pepper pieces, skin-side up, on ungreased baking sheet. Broil on top rack in oven for 10 to 15 minutes until skins are blistered and blackened. Transfer to small bowl. Cover with plastic wrap. Let sweat for about 15 minutes until cool enough to handle. Peel and discard skins (see Note). Cut into 1/3 inch (1 cm) slices. Add to rosemary mixture.

Add cheese and olive oil. Stir gently until coated. Transfer to airtight container. Marinate in refrigerator for at least 3 days to blend flavours, but no longer than 7 days. Drain and discard marinade. Makes about 2 cups (500 mL). Serves 12.

1 serving: 127 Calories; 11.1 g Total Fat (4.9 g Mono, 0.6 g Poly, 5 g Sat); 26 mg Cholesterol; 3 g Carbohydrate; trace Fibre; 4 g Protein; 327 mg Sodium

Pictured below.

Note: Prepared roasted red peppers are available in jars in most grocery stores. Drain well. Use in place of fresh, roasted red peppers.

Top: Marinated Feta, page 122
Bottom: Marinated Onion Rings, page 122

Throughout this book measurements are given in Conventional and Metric measure. To compensate for differences between the two measurements due to rounding, a full metric measure is not always used. The cup used is the standard 8 fluid ounce. Temperature is given in degrees Fahrenheit and Celsius. Baking pan measurements are in inches and centimetres as well as quarts and litres. An exact metric conversion is given on this page as well as the working equivalent (Metric Standard Measure).

Pans

Conventional – Inches	Metric – Centimetres
8 × 8 inch	20 × 20 cm
9 × 9 inch	22 × 22 cm
9 × 13 inch	22 × 33 cm
10 × 15 inch	25 × 38 cm
11 × 17 inch	28 × 43 cm
8 × 2 inch round	20 × 5 cm
9 × 2 inch round	22 × 5 cm
10 × 4 1/2 inch tube	25 × 11 cm
8 × 4 × 3 inch loaf	20 × 10 × 7.5 cm
9 × 5 × 3 inch loaf	22 × 12.5 × 7.5 cm

Oven Temperatures

Fahrenheit (°F)	Celsius (°C)	Fahrenheit (°F)	Celsius (°C)
175°	80°	350°	175°
200°	95°	375°	190°
225°	110°	400°	205°
250°	120°	425°	220°
275°	140°	450°	230°
300°	150°	475°	240°
325°	160°	500°	260°

Spoons

Conventional Measure	Metric Exact Conversion Millilitre (mL)	Metric Standard Measure Millilitre (mL)
1/8 teaspoon (tsp.)	0.6 mL	0.5 mL
1/4 teaspoon (tsp.)	1.2 mL	1 mL
1/2 teaspoon (tsp.)	2.4 mL	2 mL
1 teaspoon (tsp.)	4.7 mL	5 mL
2 teaspoons (tsp.)	9.4 mL	10 mL
1 tablespoon (tbsp.)	14.2 mL	15 mL

Cups

1/4 cup (4 tbsp.)	56.8 mL	60 mL
1/3 cup (5 1/3 tbsp.)	75.6 mL	75 mL
1/2 cup (8 tbsp.)	113.7 mL	125 mL
2/3 cup (10 2/3 tbsp.)	151.2 mL	150 mL
3/4 cup (12 tbsp.)	170.5 mL	175 mL
1 cup (16 tbsp.)	227.3 mL	250 mL
4 1/2 cups	1022.9 mL	1000 mL (1 L)

Dry Measurements

Conventional Measure Ounces (oz.)	Metric Exact Conversion Grams (g)	Metric Standard Measure Grams (g)
1 oz.	28.3 g	28 g
2 oz.	56.7 g	57 g
3 oz.	85.0 g	85 g
4 oz.	113.4 g	125 g
5 oz.	141.7 g	140 g
6 oz.	170.1 g	170 g
7 oz.	198.4 g	200 g
8 oz.	226.8 g	250 g
16 oz.	453.6 g	500 g
32 oz.	907.2 g	1000 g (1 kg)

Casseroles

Canada & Britain

Standard Size Casserole	Exact Metric Measure
1 qt. (5 cups)	1.13 L
1 1/2 qts. (7 1/2 cups)	1.69 L
2 qts. (10 cups)	2.25 L
2 1/2 qts. (12 1/2 cups)	2.81 L
3 qts. (15 cups)	3.38 L
4 qts. (20 cups)	4.5 L
5 qts. (25 cups)	5.63 L

United States

Standard Size Casserole	Exact Metric Measure
1 qt. (4 cups)	900 mL
1 1/2 qts. (6 cups)	1.35 L
2 qts. (8 cups)	1.8 L
2 1/2 qts. (10 cups)	2.25 L
3 qts. (12 cups)	2.7 L
4 qts. (16 cups)	3.6 L
5 qts. (20 cups)	4.5 L

Tip Index

Recipe Index